RETURN

OF THE

BLACKSMITHS

The Equipping Dimension Of The Apostolic

Dr. Michael Scantlebury

Foreword by
Dr. Bill Hamon

Dr. Scantlebury has taken *author's prerogative* in capitalizing certain words that are not usually capitalized according to standard grammatical practice. Also, please note that the name satan and related names are not capitalized as we choose not to acknowledge him, even to the point of disregarding standard grammatical practice.

All scripture quotations, unless otherwise indicated, are taken from the New King James Version. Copyright © 1982 by Thomas Nelson, Inc. Used by permission. All rights reserved. All scriptures marked RSV are taken from the Revised Standard Version, copyright © 1946, 1952, 1971 by the Division of Christian Education of the National Council of the Churches of Christ in the USA, and is used by permission. All scriptures marked KJV are taken from the King James Version.

Hebrew and Greek definitions are taken from James Strong, *Strong's Exhaustive Concordance of the Bible* (Peabody, MA: Hendrickson Publishers, n.d.).

Return Of The Blacksmiths – The Equipping Dimension Of The Apostolic
ISBN 1-894928-29-6
© Copyright 2003 by Michael Scantlebury

Printed by: Word Alive Press

Editorial Consultant: Amrita Bastians

Cover Design by: The Visual Limited – www.the-visual.com

TABLE OF CONTENTS

FOREWORD

Michael Scantlebury is a lover of present truth. His desire is to see Jesus Christ ministering to His Church in His full five-fold ministry of apostle, prophet, evangelist, pastor and teacher.

I can endorse this book with enthusiasm because this has been my passion and commission for many years. In the 1980's I wrote a trilogy of books on the restoration of prophets and prophetic ministry. I then wrote the book *Apostles, Prophets and the Coming Moves of God*. At the time I realized that many more books would need to be written to fully reveal and express the ministry of Jesus as Prophet and Apostle to His Church. This is one of those books.

The author uses plenty of scripture to show the scriptural validity of present-day apostles being alive and active in the Church, which is being restored to the fullness of Christ. Apostle Paul declared that Christ divided His full ministry into five equal parts. He gave names to each of these expressions of Himself: Apostle and Prophet and Evangelist and Pastor and Teacher. God is raising up men and women with the gifting of apostle and prophet. Hundreds around the world are fulfilling the ministry of apostle and prophet.

Some are called not only to be apostles but also to propagate the calling, attribute, ministry and anointing of apostles through their writing. Michael has received this calling and is fulfilling that commission through his trilogy of books on apostles and apostolic ministry. Each chapter in this book covers different aspects of the apostolic, enabling the Body of Christ to be shaped into God's divine order as a blacksmith shapes gold into a vessel of honour.

Thanks, Michael, for taking time to make this vital information and biblical truth available to members of Christ's Church. God bless you as you continue to demonstrate the ministry of the apostle through your life's ministry and writings.

Dr. Bill Hamon

Apostle/Prophet, Bishop and Founder of Christian International Ministries Network

Author of:
The Day of the Saints
Apostles, Prophets and the Coming Moves of God
Prophets and Personal Prophecy
Prophets and the Prophetic Movement
Prophets, Pitfalls and Principles
The Eternal Church

ENDORSEMENTS

Dr. Scantlebury has written a fine work on apostolic ministry. The metaphors are striking and the research solid. He has managed to demystify both the person and the calling, revealing instead the critical and practical nature of the apostolic. The maturity with which he broaches the subject adds much needed integrity to this largely underdeveloped topic. The trilogy Dr. Scantlebury has written will provide a foundational contribution to the apostolic reformation that God is bringing to His church today.

Dr. Greg Mitchell
Snr. Pastor - The River
Vancouver, BC, Canada

In every move of the Holy Spirit, God seems to raise up men and women who clearly articulate what the Spirit is doing. Michael is one of these men, raised up by the Lord for this time who has the tongue of a ready writer. May these books be used as textbooks in the training of this new breed of church leaders.

Keith Abrahams
Senior Leader: Harvest Church
Sardis, B.C., Canada

This book, the "Return of the Blacksmiths" is a timely word in the present global reformation of the Church. For saints in pursuit of where this apostolic mandate is headed, this book is destined to help reshape mentalities into the purpose and importance of the apostolic ministry, I believe a vital key conveyed in this book is that it helps to not only quicken the saints for a passion to what God is doing through His said ministries, but it also gives strong foundation that shall become a legacy for many generations.

Tim and Theresa Early
Apostle and Prophet
F.A.P. International (Ephesians 2:20)
Houston, TX, USA

It is undeniable that the greatest move of God since Martin Luther's reformation in the 1500's, is taking place in the global church. For the first time since the days of 1st century apostles, the church is recognizing, understanding and receiving the equipping dimensions of blacksmiths. No longer is the church operating or hiding in an escapist mentality. The global church is emerging into a majestic fortress, refining gold with sharpened battle axes and advancing the purposes of the Lord in all quarters. Dr Michael Scantlebury, in this volume, presents the global church with the ministry and benefits of the Blacksmith/Apostle and the emergence of governmental churches in strategic action and accurate in this present season. It is a "must read" for all kingdom people.

Dr. Robert Munien
Founder of Global Kingdom Community
Pastor of Grace Outreach International and Grace Embassy
International Based In Durban, South Africa

God's Church cannot fully function and manifest His glory without drawing from the great grace given through His Apostles. I advise every precious saint of God to not only read, but to study the book "Return Of The Blacksmiths", a seasonal book written by one of God's endtime Blacksmiths, Dr. Michael Scantlebury. I assure you that you will move in greater grace.

Apostle Jean Claude Soupin
Republic of Mauritius

The purpose and intent of God in releasing the five-fold ministry is for perfecting and edifying the saints, and to bring the Church to a position of maturity and unity. In the absence of it, the Body of Christ lies dormant and does not function in, or manifest the character, power and strength of its High Priest. As we scan the earth, some churches seem to be deficient and powerless due to doctrinal inaccuracies and more importantly, the lack of *(telios) anointing.* The church today, is a far cry from the written pattern given by God. And so we give God all the glory for men like Dr. Michael Scantlebury for this timely commentary on the Apostolic and Prophetic. This book – (The Return of the Blacksmiths– *The Equipping Dimension of the Apostolic)* will be used by God, as a tool, to stimulate inquiry and bring clarity and revelation of the intent and purposes of God and be a support to bringing the Church of God to His fullness.

Jeremiah Ransome
Snr. Elder Impact Christian Ministry
Cayman Islands

Apostle Michael Scantlebury, you've done it again! *Return of the Blacksmiths* is a wonderful addition to the reformational truths of the apostolic. While reading this book, I heard the heart beat of Christ, our Chief Apostle. *Return of the Blacksmiths* is written with great authority, yet with such clarity that anyone who reads it will be blessed! I highly recommend this book; it will strengthen and equip readers to access greater dimensions in the Lord.

Apostle Joshua Fowler
Commissioned International Church, Orlando, Florida
Author of "ACCESS GRANTED"

Return of the Blacksmiths is an extraordinary book and by far the most comprehensive exposition on the apostolic restoration that I have come across to date. As the third in the trilogy, it captures the height, breadth, and depth of this end time move of God in the *"restoration of all things"*. The revelation is excellent and the language anointed, leaving the reader with a sense of fulfillment through the discovery of these timeless, enduring and liberating truths.

This is not a quick read; instead it has to be savoured chapter by chapter. I recommend not only "The Return of the Blacksmiths" but the first two books as well, to every serious seeker of a greater understanding of who we are in Christ, and who He is in us. It is essential reading for any servant of the living God who feels called to the apostolic dimension.

Ada Thompson, M.D.
A Gathering of Eagles
Nassau, Bahamas

In his book, *Return of the Blacksmiths*, Dr. Michael Scantlebury presents a powerful look at the apostolic mandate. He takes the reader from apostolic foundations to finishing the apostolic task. Scantlebury presents a strong case for the restoration of Apostles in today's Church. An understanding of the tasks, responsibilities, difficulties and results of apostolic ministry is credentialed through scriptural examples.

I appreciate the emphasis made throughout the book on the character and lifestyle of an Apostle. These emphases are noted as being the first sign of an Apostle.

Although warfare and worship are not typically linked together, Dr. Scantlebury shows they are vital to success in accomplishing Kingdom objectives. Another emphasis made is that of unity and apostolic networks.

Reading this book will cause the reader to desire to make any changes necessary in order to be part of this mighty apostolic movement that is now occurring in the Church. Destiny awaits those willing to align with God's Apostles. They have the opportunity to become partakers of great blessings and rewards from the Lord. I recommend this book for all that are hungry to experience this fresh move of God that is taking place throughout the world today.

Barbara Wentroble
Wentroble Christian Ministries
Texas, USA

When I met Michael Scantlebury almost a decade ago, I sensed the Lord saying, "This man is a gift to the North West Region and to My Church! He carries Kingdom Keys to bless My Body." This book is full of Apostolic Wisdom. The narrative sweeps from profound Bible revelation to warm testimony. You will be stretched and challenged by this book!

Dr. John Roddam
Rector: St. Luke's Episcopal Church, Seattle, WA

I am pleased to recommend this book as a tool that would encourage and enlighten those who desire a deeper understanding of apostles and the apostolic.

Dr. David Damien
Director of Watchmen for the Nations
Port Coquitlam, BC, Canada

INTRODUCTION

" **I**f the axe is dull, And one does not sharpen the edge, Then he must use more strength; But wisdom brings success." Ecclesiastes 10:10

For centuries the Church of Jesus Christ has been using quite a bit of strength while working with a dull axe (sword, Word of God, revelation), in trying to get the job done. This has been largely due to the fact that she has been functioning without Blacksmiths (Apostles), the ones who have been graced and anointed by the Lord, with the ability to sharpen.

Actually the first metalworker mentioned in the Bible was Tubal Cain, a descendant of Cain of whom the [1]Bible said was an instructor of every craftsman in bronze and iron. In order for him to be an instructor in this field he had to learn it from his ancestor Cain, as he was the first man to [2]build an entire city named Enoch.

The Blacksmiths were the ones who worked with the metal from *foundation to finish*. This occupation included those who dug the ore from the ground, refined the metal, and worked the metal into useful objects. Refining metal was a very ancient skill, which was well developed by the time of Abraham.

Part of the refining process was, to take the metal in its raw stage through intense heat in order to get rid of all impurities, so

---

[1] Genesis 4:22
[2] Genesis 4:17

that it could then be used to make the desired product.

In the Hebrew, the word for Blacksmith is the word "*charash*" and it conveys the following meaning: charash (khaw-rash'); a primitive root; to scratch, i.e. (by implication) to engrave, plough; hence (from the use of tools) to fabricate (of any material) a fabricator or any material: artificer, carpenter, craftsman, engraver, maker, mason, skilful, smith, worker, workman, such as wrought.

In the Greek it is the word "*chalkeus*" and it conveys the following meaning: generally, worker in metal, of a goldsmith, of a worker in iron; known as a Blacksmith or smith. This word also finds its root in the word that is used to describe the Apostle Paul as a wise master *builder*. So from this we can see that functions of the Blacksmith are similar to that of the functions of the Apostle.

There is also another Greek word, "*texvitns*" which translates to the English – craftsman, artisan, designer, *architect* or workman.

This word *architect* comes from the Greek word architekton (ar-khee-tek'-tone); a chief constructor, i.e. "architect", which comes from the root word arche (ar-khay'); a commencement, or (concretely) chief (in various applications of order, time, place, or rank). This is very interesting because it carries the exact meaning for the word "*proton*" that is used when describing that "*Apostles are first*" in 1 Corinthians 12:28

"And God has appointed these in the church: *first apostles*, second prophets, third teachers, after that miracles, then gifts of healings, helps, administrations, varieties of tongues." (Italics added)

It is also used in the following texts:

"For we are God's fellow workers; you are God's field, you are God's building. According to the grace of God which was given to me, as a wise *master builder* [architect] I have laid the foundation, and another builds on it. But let each one take heed how he builds on it." 1 Corinthians 3:9-10 (Italics and Parenthesis added)

"Now, therefore, you are no longer strangers and foreigners, but fellow citizens with the saints and members of the household of God, having been built on the foundation of the apostles and prophets, Jesus Christ Himself being the chief cornerstone, in whom the whole building, being joined together, grows into a holy temple in the Lord, in whom you also are being built together for a dwelling place of God in the Spirit." Ephesians 2:19-22

As was previously mentioned, the Blacksmiths were the ones who worked with the metal from *foundation to finish*. In a similar manner, the Apostles are to work on the "Church" from *foundation to finish*. Some would have us to believe that Apostles are not required today, on the surmise that their responsibility was to write the original scriptures and once that was completed; the Apostles were to be done away with. However, as we would see in Chapter One and beyond, this is only a presumption and not fact.

The Blacksmiths/Apostles are being restored, and we are beginning to see the emergence of a powerful, new Church rising in the earth! The earth shall indeed be filled with the *knowledge* of the glory of the Lord as the waters cover the sea. Hallelujah!

This book is the third in the trilogy of books on the apostolic; the first was "Five Pillars Of the Apostolic – Towards A Mature Church" and the second was "Apostolic Purity – In Pursuit of His Excellence".

It is my prayer that you would be blessed reading this book as I was in writing it.

Dr. Michael Scantlebury
Founder and Apostle
Dominion-Life International Ministries

CHAPTER 1

IN DEFENCE OF APOSTLES TODAY

I would like to dedicate the first chapter of this book to those of you who may have picked it up, because of the title *"Return Of The Blacksmiths – The Equipping Dimension of The Apostolic"* or because you loved the cover design, but do not believe or accept that there are Apostles today in the Body of Christ.

If you belong to any one of these categories, I encourage you to take the time to read this chapter, but only after you have laid aside any pre-conceived notions concerning the issue of present-day Apostles.

I will set out to show, from the Scriptures, that there were in fact many more Apostles in the early Church than the original twelve who walked with Jesus and Matthias (who was Judas' replacement).

However, before beginning that exercise let me first provide a definition for the word "Apostle". Our English word "Apostle" comes from the Greek verb *apostello,* which means, "*sent one*". However, it is implied that one is sent and commissioned by the sender to a particular task, or with a specific purpose. When this is done, "the emissary" or "sent one" has full authority and acts as an ambassador of the one "sending him." In the original usage, the Greeks used this word *apostello* in a stronger and spiritual sense to denote that the one being sent was done with a sense of divine authorization.

One of the best examples of this apostolic/sent one dimension is found in the gospel account of Matthew where we read the following:

"And when He had called His twelve *disciples* to Him, He gave them power over unclean spirits, to cast them out, and to heal all kinds of sickness and all kinds of disease. Now the names of the twelve *Apostles* are these: first, Simon, who is called Peter, and Andrew his brother; James the son of Zebedee, and John his brother; Philip and Bartholomew; Thomas and Matthew the tax collector; James the son of Alphaeus, and Lebbaeus, whose surname was Thaddaeus; Simon the Cananite, and Judas Iscariot, who also betrayed Him. These twelve Jesus *sent out and commanded them, saying:* 'Do not go into the way of the Gentiles, and do not enter a city of the Samaritans. But go rather to the lost sheep of the house of Israel. *And as you go, preach, saying, The kingdom of heaven is at hand. Heal the sick, cleanse the lepers, raise the dead, cast out demons. Freely you have received freely give. Provide neither gold nor silver nor copper in your money belts. Nor bag for your journey, nor two tunics, nor sandals, nor staffs; for a worker is worthy of his food.* Now whatever city or town you enter, *inquire who in it is worthy,* and stay there till you go out. And when you go into a household, greet it. *If the household is worthy, let your peace come upon it.*

But if it is not worthy, let your peace return to you. And whoever will not receive you nor hear your words, when you depart from that house or city, shake off the dust from your feet. Assuredly, I say to you, it will be more tolerable for the land of Sodom and Gomorrah in the day of judgement than for that city!'" Matthew 10:1-15 (Italics added).

Principles Set By Jesus
From Disciple To Apostle: Matthew 10:1-2

Verse 1 declares that Jesus calls His twelve, *"disciples"*. Disciples in the Greek is the word "mathetes" which means, pupil or learner – and in verse 2 they are called Apostles - "apostolos" (ap-os-tol-oss), and as was said before, in the Greek it conveys the following meaning: "A special messenger, delegate, one commissioned for a particular task or role, one who is sent forth with a message. One who is sent to represent another in the power and authority of the one who sent him/her."

So quintessentially, the disciples became Apostles as they were sent and commissioned, and given a mandate with the corresponding authority, for its fulfillment. This is the first place we see the Apostles emerging. In the study of scriptures, there is a principle, which is known as the *"first mention principle"* or *"law of first mention"*. This is a principle by which the interpretation of any verse is aided by considering the first time its subject appears in Scripture. In general, the first time a point is mentioned in Scripture, it carries with it a meaning, which will be consistent throughout the entire Bible.

In light of this, the principle surrounding Apostles and apostolic ministry will be consistent throughout scripture:

Apostolic Reference In Scripture

When the Church was being established it was done upon the foundation laid by the Apostles and Prophets [Ephesians 2:20]. Most people believe that the death of the early Apostles and

Prophets meant that it was the end of Apostles and Prophets in the body of Christ. However, a thorough search of the scriptures establishes the fact, that there were more Apostles than the original twelve. For a brief look we can cite the following scriptures:

"Moreover, brethren, I declare to you that the gospel which I preached to you, which also you received and in which you stand, by which also you are saved, if you hold fast that word which I preached to you – unless you believed in vain. For I delivered to you first of all that which I also received; that Christ died for our sins according to the scriptures, And that He was buried, and that He rose again the third day according to the Scriptures, And that He was seen by Cephas, *then by the twelve* [that is the original twelve Apostles]. After that He was seen by over five hundred brethren at once, of whom the greater part remain to the present, but some have fallen asleep. After that He was seen by James, *then by all the Apostles* [I submit to you that this was referring to the other Apostles, apart from the original twelve]. Then last of all He was seen by me also, as by one born out of due time." 1 Corinthians 15:1–8 (Italics and Parenthesis added)

"The Twelve" is a regular designation of the Apostles in the Gospels, and the Apostle Paul uses it in 1 Corinthians 15:5. Its symbolic appropriateness is obvious, and recurs in such places as Revelation 21:14. The whole Matthias incident in Acts 1:15-26 is concerned with making up the number of the Twelve. Yet Apostle Paul's consciousness of apostleship is equally clear as he makes reference time and time again in most of his writings[3]. Barnabas is called an Apostle[4], and is introduced by Apostle Paul into an argument that denies any qualitative difference between his own Apostleship and that of the Twelve[5]. Yet still, there were many more Apostles mentioned in the Scriptures, whom we will identify later on in this chapter.

Along with Paul and the other Apostles referred to in the preceding Scriptural text, there have been many other Apostles released into the body of Christ, since then. Let us now take a look at Ephesians chapter four, from which some very salient points can be extracted:

> "But to each one of us grace was given according to the measure of Christ's gift. Therefore He says: "When He ascended on high, He led captivity captive, And *gave gifts to men*." (Now this, "He ascended"—what does it mean but that He also first descended into the lower parts of the earth? He who descended is also the One who ascended far above all the heavens, that He might fill all things.) *And He Himself gave some to be apostles*, some prophets, some evangelists, and some pastors and teachers, *for the equipping of the saints for the work of ministry, for the edifying of the body of Christ, till we all come to the unity of the faith and of the knowledge of the Son of God, to a perfect man, to the measure of the stature of the fullness of Christ;* that we should no longer be children, tossed to and fro and carried about with every wind of doctrine, by the trickery of men, in the cunning craftiness of deceitful plotting, but, speaking the truth in love, may grow up in all things into Him who is the head— Christ— from whom the whole body, joined and knit together by what every joint supplies, according to the effective working by which every part does its share, causes growth of the body for the edifying of itself in love." Ephesians 4:7–16 (Italics added)

Points To Extract From Ephesians 4:7–16
* Jesus Himself gave the ministry gifts of Apostles, prophets, evangelists, pastors and teachers to men.

---

3 1 Corinthians 1:1; 2 Corinthians 1:1; Galatians 1:1; Ephesians 1:1; Colossians 1:1; 1 Timothy 1:1; 2 Timothy 1:1; Titus 1:1

4 Acts 14:4, 14

5 1 Corinthians 9:1-6

- These gifts were given to His Body, the Church.

- They were given for several reasons:
    a. For equipping the saints in His body

    b. To allow the saints to do the work of the ministry

    c. For the edifying of the body of Christ

- The ministry gifts were to function in the body of Christ for a specific time period, until the following happens:
    a. We all come into the unity of the faith

    b. We all come into the knowledge of the Son of God

    c. We all come into a perfect man, to the measure of the stature of the fullness of Christ

    d. We are no longer children, tossed to and fro and carried about with every wind of doctrine

    e. We speak the truth in love and grow up in all things into Him who is the head, Christ.

Evidently, these things have not yet been fulfilled in the body of Christ. Therefore the ministry gifts are still in operation, with specific emphasis conferred upon that of the Apostle. However, I would like to highlight the aspect of the Church coming into a *"perfect man."*

The word *"perfect"* is from the Greek word *teleios,* which is rendered *"complete"*. This comes from the root word *telos* or *tello,* which means "to set out for a definite point or goal; the conclusion of an act or state; result; purpose."

Therefore, for anyone to refuse apostolic ministry in the Church is to seek to deny the means by which Jesus has ordained, for His Church to be perfected. As we look at the following verses of scripture, it is evident that in order for the Church to be all that the Lord intended, we need the continued ministry of Apostles.

Ephesians 2: 19-22
"Now, therefore, you are no longer strangers and foreigners, but fellow citizens with the saints and members of the household of God, *having been built on the foundation of the apostles and prophets, Jesus Christ Himself being the chief cornerstone*, in whom the whole building, being joined together, grows into a holy temple in the Lord, in whom you also are being built together for a dwelling place of God in the Spirit." (Italics added)

We would all agree that the Church of Jesus is still being built and as such, the foundation and that of the Cornerstone is still very much in use.

The Cornerstone is what determined the dimensions of the building. In those days there were no elaborate plans as we have today, and hence the cornerstone was used to determine the height, size, shape, etc of the building to be constructed. So the main task of the Apostles and prophets is to bring revelation of Christ to His Church, which is still under construction! Growth can only take place to the degree of the *Revelation* we have of Christ. "Faith comes by hearing the Word of God".

1 Corinthians 3: 9-14
"For we are God's fellow workers; you are God's field, you are God's building. According to the grace of God which was given to me, as a wise master builder I have laid the foundation, and another builds on it. But let each one take heed how he builds on it. For no other foundation can anyone lay than that which is laid, which is Jesus Christ. Now if anyone builds on this foundation with gold, silver, precious stones, wood, hay, straw, each one's

work will become clear; for the Day will declare it, because it will be revealed by fire; and the fire will test each one's work, of what sort it is. If anyone's work which he has built on it endures, he will receive a reward."

The Foundation that the Apostles lay is Jesus Christ, Himself! So the foundation that our lives are built upon is the revelation of Christ, and that is the function or grace that has been given to the Apostles and prophets.

However, please note that Apostles and prophets are not only to lay the foundation, but are also being used to construct the building; in essence, they are to work from *start to finish*! According to *Ephesians 4: 11-13* they are *to exist until* the Church God is building, reaches maturity or completion or per-fection!

"And God has *appointed* [placed with permanence] these *in the church: first apostles*, second prophets, third teach-ers, after that miracles, then gifts of healings, helps, administrations, varieties of tongues." 1 Corinthians 12:28 (Italics and Parenthesis added)

God has "*appointed*" or "*set*" these in the church! That word appointed or set in the Greek carries the meaning of "*set or placed with a sense of permanence*". So essentially, God has permanently placed in the Church, Apostles. There has always been, and there will always be Apostles in the Church of Jesus Christ!

I like what Rick Joyner said in his writing on "The Foundation": "Paul wasn't just trying to get people to confess Jesus as their Saviour, though that is certainly an important beginning. He wasn't just trying to get them to understand Christian doctrine accurately, though that too is important. This was also about much more than just planting churches wherever he went. All of these were but a means to the end — having each believer, *conformed to the image of Christ*. This is the image of God that many were originally created to bear. This begins with reconciliation to God through the atonement of the cross. After the atonement comes the renewing of our minds, and the conforming of our lives to His ways.

God does not judge the condition or quality of His Church by how good the meetings are on Sunday morning, but by how good the people are on Monday morning. The main calling upon our lives is more than just knowing the truth - it is having that truth become our life.

The main purpose of the church is more than just providing ministry to the people—it is labouring until each one is conformed to the image of Christ. That is the foundation of apostolic and prophetic ministry, and what they are called to impart to all of the ministries in the church. This is the foundation of ministry, labouring for each one to be made complete in Christ."

OTHER APOSTLES BESIDES THE ORIGINAL TWELVE

The New Testament uses *apostolos* for the twelve Apostles chosen personally by Jesus. They are the ones with whom we are most familiar, but they are not the only ones. At least twelve others are also called "Apostle" in the New Testament.

Some contend that the only other Apostles referred to in scripture were Matthias and Paul. In their debate they conclude that Paul was the Divine choice to replace Judas in the original twelve. It is said that the process for choosing Matthias was a flawed process of voting, and as such the Lord had to intervene and call Paul. They validate their line of reasoning by the fact that Matthias was never once mentioned again in scripture after they voted him in.

Let's take a journey into the pages of scripture to see what it says on this very important issue:

PAUL – He was not one of the original twelve and had no problem calling himself, and others, Apostles. In most of his letters he begins with this proclamation: "Paul, called to be an Apostle of Jesus Christ through the will of God." 1 Corinthians 1:1. (Emphasis added) You can check through many of his other [6]letters and see this same proclamation.

Interestingly, even though Paul was not one of the original twelve, the Lord used him to write almost the whole New Testament I wonder *why*? It would seem as though the Lord was indeed showing that His Church had to be built on *"revelation knowledge"*. This was the same Paul who declared – "But I make known to you, brethren, that *the gospel which was preached by me* is not according to man. For *I neither received it from man, nor was I taught it, but it came through the revelation of Jesus Christ.*" Galatians 1:11-12 (Italics added)

JAMES THE LORD'S BROTHER

"Then after three years I went up to Jerusalem to see Peter, and remained with him fifteen days. But I saw none of the other apostles except James, the Lord's brother." Galatians 1:18-19

Please note, that not only was he not one of the original twelve Apostles but he did not even believe in Jesus his brother, when He walked the earth:

"After these things Jesus walked in Galilee; for He did not want to walk in Judea, because the Jews sought to kill Him. Now the Jews' Feast of Tabernacles was at hand. His brothers therefore said to Him, "Depart from here and go into Judea, that Your disciples also may see the works that You are doing. For no one does anything in secret while he himself seeks to be known openly. If You do these things, show Yourself to the world." *For even*

---

[6] 2 Corinthians 1:1, Galatians 1:1, Ephesians 1:1, Colossians 1:1,
1 Timothy 1:1, 2 Timothy 1:1 and Titus 1:1

His brothers did not believe in Him." John 7: 1-5 (Italics added)

However, he had a personal visitation from Jesus and obviously got saved, and was given an apostolic call and commissioning:

"Moreover, brethren, I declare to you the gospel which I preached to you, which also you received and in which you stand, by which also you are saved, if you hold fast that word which I preached to you—unless you believed in vain. For I delivered to you first of all that which I also received: that Christ died for our sins according to the Scriptures, and that He was buried, and that He rose again the third day according to the Scriptures, and that *He was seen by Cephas, then by the twelve.* After that He was seen by over five hundred brethren at once, of whom the greater part remain to the present, but some have fallen asleep. *After that He was seen by James, then by all the apostles.* Then last of all He was seen by me also, as by one born out of due time. For I am the least of the apostles, who am not worthy to be called an apostle, because I persecuted the church of God." 1 Corinthians 15:1-9 (Italics added)

THEN BY ALL THE APOSTLES – Who are they? I do not believe that he is speaking about the twelve, otherwise he would have said so, just as he did in verse five! This must be speaking about a much wider group of Apostles!

BARNABAS – He was the one who took on the arduous task of introducing the Apostle Paul (then Saul) to the church, as most of the early believers were afraid of him because of his previous track record of killing Believers.

"Now it happened in Iconium that they went together to the synagogue of the Jews, and so spoke that a great multitude both of the Jews and of the Greeks believed. But the unbelieving Jews stirred up the Gentiles and poisoned their minds against the brethren. Therefore they stayed there a long time, speaking boldly in the Lord, who was bearing witness to the word of His grace, granting signs and wonders to be done by their hands. *But the multitude of the city was divided: part sided with the Jews, and part with the apostles."* Acts 14:1-4 (Italics added)

Here we see the scripture speaking about the city of Iconium being divided between the Jews and the *Apostles*; this begs the question – who were these *Apostles* that the scripture was making reference to? The answer can be found later in the same passage:

"Now when the people saw what Paul had done, they raised their voices, saying in the Lycaonian language, "The gods have come down to us in the likeness of men!" And Barnabas they called Zeus, and Paul, Hermes, because he was the chief speaker. Then the priest of Zeus, whose temple was in front of their city, brought oxen and garlands to the gates, intending to sacrifice with the multitudes. *But when the apostles Barnabas and Paul* heard this, they tore their clothes and ran in among the multitude, crying out and saying, "Men, why are you doing these things? We also are men with the same nature as you, and preach to you that you should turn from these useless things to the living God, who made the heaven, the earth, the sea, and all things that are in them, who in bygone generations allowed all nations to walk in their own ways. Nevertheless He did not leave Himself without witness, in that He did good, gave us rain from heaven and fruitful seasons, filling our hearts with food and gladness." Acts 14: 11-17 (Italics added)

Here, the scripture clearly reveals to us that Barnabas was referred to, as an Apostle. Barnabas is again referred to in the following passage, making it abundantly clear that he was indeed an Apostle:

"Am I not an apostle? Am I not free? Have I not seen Jesus Christ our Lord? Are you not my work in the Lord? If I am not an apostle to others, yet doubtless I am to you. For you are the seal of my apostleship in the Lord. My defence to those who examine me is this: Do we have no right to eat and drink? Do we have no right to take along a believing wife, *as do also the other apostles, the brothers of the Lord, and Cephas? Or is it only Barnabas and I* who have no right to refrain from working?" 1 Corinthians 9:1-6 (Italics added)

Here the Apostle Paul is making a defence of his benefits as an Apostle. He makes reference to several who were also Apostles; the brothers of the Lord, Cephas and of course Barnabus. (His reference to brothers is interesting; implying that more than one of Jesus' brothers were Apostles). So far we made reference to James but now Paul is alluding to more.

APOLLOS – Here is another young man whom the Apostle Paul places alongside as a fellow Apostle. He was a learned Jew who was very eloquent in the scripture, but he only knew the baptism of John and he submitted himself to Aquilla and Priscilla, who expounded him more thoroughly in the scriptures.

"Now these things, brethren, I have figuratively transferred *to myself and Apollos* for your sakes, that you may learn in us not to think beyond what is written, that none of you may be puffed up on behalf of one against the other. For who makes you differ from another? And what do you have that you did not receive? Now if you did indeed receive it, why do you boast as if you had not received it? You are already full! You are already rich!

You have reigned as kings without us—and indeed I could wish you did reign, that we also might reign with you! For I think that *God has displayed us, the apostles,* last, as men condemned to death; for we have been made a spectacle to the world, both to angels and to men." 1 Corinthians 4:6-9 (Italics added)

ANDRONICUS – An Apostle from Rome.
"Greet *Andronicus and Junia,* my countrymen and my fellow prisoners, *who are of note among the apostles,* who also were in Christ before me." Romans 16:7 (Italics added)

"Of note among the apostles" – suggest that there were several, at least in Rome.

JUNIA – An Apostle from Rome of the same calibre as Andronicus. There is some suggestion that this was a woman, and as such, a female Apostle. The scope of this writing however, is not to debate if there is/were female Apostles. The scope of this writing is to prove that there are/were other Apostles apart from the original twelve. See Romans 16:7

SILVANUS/SILAS – This was the young man that Paul chose as his traveling companion, after he and Barnabas had a heated disagreement over the inclusion of John Mark on their traveling team, after he deserted them on an earlier mission. Paul describes him as an Apostle in the following passage:

"Paul, Silvanus, and Timothy, To the church of the Thessalonians in God the Father and the Lord Jesus Christ: Grace to you and peace from God our Father and the Lord Jesus Christ. We give thanks to God always for you all, making mention of you in our prayers," 1 Thessalonians 1:1-2 (Italics added)

"For you yourselves know, brethren, *that our* coming to

you was not in vain. But even after we had suffered before and were spitefully treated at Philippi, as you know, *we were* bold in our God to speak to you the gospel of God in much conflict. For *our exhortation* did not come from error or uncleanness, nor was it in deceit. But as *we have been approved by God to be entrusted with the gospel*, even so we speak, not as pleasing men, but God who tests our hearts. For neither at any time did *we use* flattering words, as you know, nor a cloak for covetousness—God is witness. Nor did *we seek* glory from men, either from you or from others, when *we might have made demands as apostles of Christ*." 1 Thessalonians 2:1-6 (Italics added)

It is quite evident that the Apostle Paul was referring to himself, Silas and Timothy as Apostles of Jesus Christ.

TIMOTHY – He was the young Apostle referred to in the preceding scriptural text and the same individual that was established as the bishop over the churches in Asia with his home base at Ephesus. It is very interesting to note that his [7]father was a Greek, and an unbeliever, and was raised up in his Christian heritage by his believing [8]mother and grandmother.

EPAPHRODITUS – He is referred to as *"a messenger"* (translated from the Greek word apostolos – English Apostle) to the Philippians' church. In the Revised Version of the Bible it is rendered *"your apostle"* in the margin of the following text:

"Yet I considered it necessary to send to you Epaph roditus, my brother, fellow worker, and fellow soldier, but *your messenger* [Apostle] and the one who ministered to my need…" Philippians 2:25 (Italics and Parenthesis added)

---

[7] Acts 16:1-3

[8] 1 Timothy 1:5

UNNAMED APOSTLES – This text is similar to the preceding text in that some unnamed brethren are described as *"messengers of the churches"* (translated from the Greek word apostolos – English Apostle). However, the Revised Version renders them as "apostles of the churches" in the margin of the following text:

> "If anyone inquires about Titus, he is my partner and fellow worker concerning you. Or *if our brethren are inquired about, they are messengers* [Apostles] *of the churches*, the glory of Christ." 2 Corinthians 8:23 (Italics and Parenthesis added)

We have to also look at the fact that Paul spoke about "false apostles". The very fact that he (Paul) found it necessary to denounce certain persons as "false apostles, deceitful workers, fashioning themselves into Apostles of Christ" (11:13) shows that there was no thought in the primitive church of restricting the apostleship to a body of 12 or 13 men. "Had the number been definitely restricted, the claims of these interlopers would have been self-condemned" (Lightfoot, Galatians, 97).

> *"For I consider that I am not at all inferior to the most eminent apostles.* Even though I am untrained in speech, yet I am not in knowledge. But we have been thoroughly manifested among you in all things. Did I commit sin in humbling myself that you might be exalted, because I preached the gospel of God to you free of charge? I robbed other churches, taking wages from them to minister to you. And when I was present with you, and in need, I was a burden to no one, for what I lacked the brethren who came from Macedonia supplied. And in everything I kept myself from being burdensome to you, and so I will keep myself. As the truth of Christ is in me, no one shall stop me from this boasting in the regions of Achaia. Why? Because I do not love you? God knows!

But what I do, I will also continue to do, that I may cut off the opportunity from those who desire an opportunity to be regarded just as we are in the things of which they boast. *For such are false apostles, deceitful workers, transforming themselves into apostles of Christ.* And no wonder! For satan himself transforms himself into an angel of light. Therefore it is no great thing if his ministers also transform themselves into ministers of righteousness, whose end will be according to their works." 2 Corinthians 11:5-15 (Italics added)

Again, let me re-emphasize. The fact that Paul had to make such a stinging defence of his apostleship and judge others by his quality and standard, is sufficient proof that not only were there false apostles in his time, but true, legitimate Apostles other than the original twelve. Therefore it is quite clear, and evident, that the same way evangelists, pastors and teachers are still operative and functional in the Body of Christ today, it must be no different when it comes to prophets and Apostles. They must be accepted as needed and relevant today, if the Church is to come into full maturity.

Please understand that part of the technology that operates in the ministry gift of the Apostle, is the ability to decode the mysteries of Christ. They are given the ability by the Lord to bring clarity to some of the scriptures that have been hidden or sealed up, until the time appointed for their unveiling. For example when the Lord spoke to both Daniel, as recorded in the book of Daniel, and John in the book of Revelation, He declared to them:

"Then it happened, when I, Daniel, had seen the vision and was seeking the meaning, that suddenly there stood before me one having the appearance of a man. And I heard a man's voice between the banks of the Ulai, who called, and said, "Gabriel, make this man understand the vision." So he came near where I stood, and when he came I was afraid and fell on my face; but he said to me,

"Understand, son of man, that the vision refers to the time of the end."... And the vision of the evenings and mornings Which was told is true; *Therefore seal up the vision, For it refers to many days in the future.*" And I, Daniel, fainted and was sick for days; afterward I arose and went about the king's business. I was astonished by the vision, but no one understood it." Daniel 8:15-18, 26-27 (Italics added)

"Now when the seven thunders uttered their voices, I was about to write; but I heard a voice from heaven saying to me, *"Seal up the things which the seven thunders uttered, and do not write them."* The angel whom I saw standing on the sea and on the land raised up his hand to heaven and swore by Him who lives forever and ever, who created heaven and the things that are in it, the earth and the things that are in it, and the sea and the things that are in it, that there should be delay no longer, but in the days of the sounding of the seventh angel, when he is about to sound, the mystery of God would be finished, *as He declared to His servants the prophets.*" Revelation 10:4-7 (Italics added)

There were certain things that John had to seal up, which God would have declared to His servants the prophets. This is very significant, as God has graced Apostles with the ability to decode and declare the fulfillment or appointed timing of things that were prophesied by the prophets.

Daniel can be used as an example of this apostolic dimension as recorded in the following:

"In the first year of Darius the son of Ahasuerus, of the lineage of the Medes, who was made king over the realm of the Chaldeans—in the first year of his reign *I, Daniel, understood by the books the number of the years specified by the word of the LORD through Jeremiah the prophet, that He would accomplish seventy years in the desolations of Jerusalem."* Daniel 9:1-2 (Italics added)

Here we read that Daniel was able to understand and decode the timing of the prophetic word spoken by the prophet Jeremiah. He then sets about to see this word come to pass, and as we read on in the book, the Lord does answer his prayer and brings fulfillment to the prophetic word.

We also see this apostolic dimension wonderfully demonstrated in the book of Acts:

"Now when the Day of Pentecost had fully come, they were all with one accord in one place. And suddenly there came a sound from heaven, as of a rushing mighty wind, and it filled the whole house where they were sitting. Then there appeared to them divided tongues, as of fire, and one sat upon each of them. *And they were all filled with the Holy Spirit and began to speak with other tongues, as the Spirit gave them utterance.* And there were dwelling in Jerusalem Jews, devout men, from every nation under heaven. And when this sound occurred, the multitude came together, and were confused, because everyone heard them speak in his own language. *Then they were all amazed and marvelled, saying to one another, "Look, are not all these who speak Galileans? And how is it that we hear, each in our own language in which we were born?* Parthians and Medes and Elamites, those dwelling in Mesopotamia, Judea and Cappadocia, Pontus and Asia, Phrygia and Pamphylia, Egypt and the parts of Libya adjoining Cyrene, visitors from Rome, both Jews and proselytes, Cretans and Arabs—we hear them speaking in our own tongues the wonderful works of God." *So they were all amazed and perplexed, saying to one another, "Whatever could this mean?" Others mocking said, "They are full of new wine. But Peter, standing up* with the eleven, *raised his voice and said* to them, "Men of Judea and all who dwell in Jerusalem, let this be known to you, and heed my words. For these are not drunk, as you suppose, since it is only the third hour of the day. *But this is what was spoken by the prophet Joel:*" Acts 2:1-16 (Italics added)

This is very powerful; here we see the emergence of the Promise of the Father resulting in the Apostles speaking in tongues they never learned. The Jews were confused and astonished at this incident, and not knowing what to make of it, assumed they were drunk on a new wine that was just released into the market. At this point, the Apostle Peter gets a divine revelation of what was happening. He was given the ability to decode the mystery that was taking place. He declared, *"This is what was spoken by the prophet Joel"* – how did he know this, when everyone else around him were astonished and confused? I declare to you, that it was the very same way he understood that[9] *"Jesus was the Christ the Son of the living God"*, by divine revelation. Flesh and blood did not reveal it to him but the Father who is in heaven.

There is need for this dimension to continue in the Church of Jesus Christ in the earth today. We need Apostles who have this grace upon their lives to assist in decoding the mysteries of God. They are to be fully released and accepted in the Body of Christ so that they can lend support in the perfecting of the saints, in order to accomplish the work of the ministry intended by the Lord.

Note of Interest – in Revelation 18:20, when Babylon is finally destroyed, a command goes out for Apostles and prophets to rejoice! More on the restoration of Apostles to the Body of Christ can be read in my books "Five Pillars of the Apostolic" and "Apostolic Purity" (ordering details at the end of this book).

---

[9] Matthew 16:16

CHAPTER 2

WORKING WITH GOLD

B ang! Bang! Bang! Is the sound being heard as the Blacksmith works arduously at his task of shaping and forming the lump of refined gold into a predetermined vessel.

Job 23:10 declares, "When He has tested me, I shall come forth as gold." This perfectly describes what the Lord is seeking to do through His Apostles in this hour. He is restoring them as "Spirit-Filled" Blacksmiths with one purpose in mind, that of assisting in the "*perfecting*" of His people into the predetermined measure and stature of Christ.

While my profession in the natural is not that of a Blacksmith, I have been reading on how gold is refined and then hammered into usefulness. Permit me to share some truths that I have gleaned.

As we press deeper into the Twenty-First Century and the

imminent return of our Lord, Jesus Christ, there is a dimension to the *"baptism of fire"* that God is releasing, to refine and purify His people in this hour. The Word of God is littered with reference to the great refining and purifying that would be done before Jesus returns. Here are just a few of them - John the Baptist declared:

> "I indeed baptize you with water unto repentance, but He who is coming after me is mightier than I, whose sandals I am not worthy to carry, He will baptize you with the Holy Spirit *and fire*. His winnowing fan is in His hand, and He will thoroughly clean out His threshing floor, and gather His wheat into the barn; but He will burn up the chaff with unquenchable fire." Matthew 3:11-12 (Italics added)

Four hundred years before the writings of the New Testament, the Prophet Malachi declared the following in his prophetic writings:

> "He will *sit as a refiner and a purifier* of silver; He will *purify* the sons of Levi, And *purge* them as gold and silver, That *they may offer to the LORD An offering in righteousness*." Malachi 3:3 (Italics added)

The Apostle John Declared The Following:
"Behold what manner of love the Father has bestowed on us, that we should be called children of God! Therefore the world does not know us, because it did not know Him. Beloved, now we are children of God; and it has not yet been revealed what we shall be, but we know that when He is revealed, we shall be like Him, for we shall see Him as He is. And everyone who has this hope in Him *purifies himself, just as He is pure*." 1 John 3:1-3 (Italics added)

The Apostle Paul Puts It This Way:
"But we all, with unveiled face, beholding as in a mirror

the glory of the Lord, *are being transformed into the same image from glory to glory,* just as by the Spirit of the Lord." 2 Corinthians 3:18 (Italics added)

In many places, the people of God are crying out for His Manifested Presence. Fed-up with mere programs, activities and shallow religious works, Spirit-Filled Saints of God from every nation are storming heaven and proclaiming that "*the knowledge of the Glory of God must cover the earth, as the waters cover the sea.*" However, as the Lord responds, He is causing a powerful purifying and refining to take place with the saints, just as it is recorded in the book of Malachi:

"Behold, I send My messenger, and he will prepare the way before Me. And *the Lord, whom you seek, will suddenly come* to His temple, even the Messenger of the covenant, in whom you delight. Behold, He is coming, says the Lord of hosts. But who can endure the day of His coming? And who can stand when He appears? For He is like a *refiner's fire* and like launderers' soap. He will sit as a *refiner and a purifier of silver;* He will *purify the sons of Levi, and purge them as gold and silver,* that they may offer to the Lord an offering in righteousness." Malachi 3:1-3 (Italics added)

The word refine is the Hebrew word "tsaraph"; and is rendered - to melt; refine; test or purify, with regards to metals - it also carries the idea of any kind of refining, whether literal or figurative. It also refers to the melting process whereby impurities are removed from precious metals, such as gold and silver.

In the Greek it is the word "puroomai" and is rendered – to burn or refine with regards to metals. It is the same word that is used in Revelation 3:18 – "I counsel you to buy from Me gold *refined* in the fire, that you may be rich;" (Italics added).

It is interesting to note that the Lord was speaking to the

angel of the church of the Laodiceans (to whom most, if not all, Bible scholars and laymen alike agree, refers to the Church and age in which we now live). Rich and increased with natural wealth and goods, she has become very lukewarm and does not realize her nakedness. A cry goes forth from the heart of the Father to become either hot or cold, to avoid having Him spew her out of His mouth. He then declares that she should go and *purchase, with her accumulated wealth "gold that has been refined in the fire"*! This is the reason for the return of the Blacksmiths [Apostles] so that we can all become "*refined and beaten gold*"

"And to the angel of the church of the Laodiceans write, 'These things says the Amen, the Faithful and True Witness, the Beginning of the creation of God: "I know your works, that you are neither cold nor hot. I could wish you were cold or hot. So then, because you are lukewarm, and neither cold nor hot, I will vomit you out of My mouth. Because you say, 'I am rich, have become wealthy, and have need of nothing'—and do not know that you are wretched, miserable, poor, blind, and naked—*I counsel you to buy from Me gold refined in the fire, that you may be rich;* and white garments, that you may be clothed, that the shame of your nakedness may not be revealed; and anoint your eyes with eye salve, that you may see. As many as I love, I rebuke and chasten. Therefore be zealous and repent. Behold, I stand at the door and knock. If anyone hears My voice and opens the door, I will come in to him and dine with him, and he with Me. To him who overcomes I will grant to sit with Me on My throne, as I also overcame and sat down with My Father on His throne. He who has an ear, let him hear what the Spirit says to the churches." Revelation 3:14-22 (Italics added)

Buy Gold, Refined In The Fire? Yes! - Refining Gold

It is my understanding, that in ancient days the refiner would sit before the crucible, fixing his eye on the metal. He would do this to ensure that the heat was not too intense that it would destroy the metal, but that it remained in the fire at the right degree of heat, for the exact period of time.

The refiner knew exactly when the precious metal was ready, and that was when he saw his own image reflected in the glowing mass. At that precise moment he knew the dross was completely removed, and his task was accomplished.

In like manner, our heavenly Refiner is sitting as our Purifier, waiting to see His Image reflected in us:

"But He knows the way that I take; When He has tested me, I shall come forth as gold." Job 23:10

"The refining pot is for silver and the furnace for gold, But the LORD tests the hearts." Proverbs 17:3

"Behold, I have refined you, but not as silver; I have tested you in the furnace of affliction." Isaiah 48:10

"For they indeed for a few days chastened us as seemed best to them, but He for our profit, that we may be partakers of His holiness. Now no chastening seems to be joyful for the present, but painful; nevertheless, afterward it yields the peaceable fruit of righteousness to those who have been trained by it." Hebrews 12:10-11

Have you been experiencing the Lord in this way? Have you been feeling the sense of a deep work being done in your heart? Rejoice, because the Refiner is at work, making you ready for the next and final phase so that He can shine through you to the utmost!

As soon as the raw gold has been refined, the Blacksmith takes it to the next stage. [10]Bang! The iron hammer of the smith

---

[10] Excerpt taken from and used by permission from a writing titled "Beaten Gold" by Bryan Huppert of www.SheepTrax.com

is raised and brought down on the lump of freshly mined gold. Soon the gold begins to *"suffer"* many things at the smiths' hands. The gold, being very malleable, is squashed a bit, contorted, misshapen, and is soon hit again, and again, and again.

The gold is on an anvil, a hard place, where it is beaten torturously and in great agony until it takes on a shape it was not. It is pressed beyond endurance, beyond its limits, beyond its natural threshold of pain until it is no longer recognizable as a lump, but only as gold. The very crystalline structure of the gold is changing and hardening. The Blacksmith continues to rain blow upon blow on the gold, hammering away, seemingly without mercy.

The gold can only feel the pain, feel the unfairness of the circumstance, feel the sting of the hammer. The Blacksmith, through eyes of faith, can see the thing of beauty and service that he is making, as he applies one crushing blow at a time.

Gold is a biblical symbol for God's nature. He says that the gold and silver are His - gold speaking of deity and silver speaking of redemption and salvation. The Bible, in many places, uses a peculiar phrase called "beaten gold".

The only gold used in the construction of [11]Moses' Tabernacle was beaten gold. When Solomon built the Temple and his own house, enormous amounts of gold were used. Please understand that it is only beaten gold that enters into divine service.

Beaten gold was made by hammering it into very fine sheets, which were then folded over and beaten again and again until it reached the consistency required by the Blacksmith. The Blacksmith works, seeing the end from the beginning. With his eyes all he sees is a lump of gold before him, but with his mind he sees it being forged into a vessel of honour, fit for the Kings service.

---

[11] Exodus chapters 36-37 read and see the extensive use of "beaten gold".

When we come to Christ, we are like a new lump of gold, mined from the mud pits of the world. We are born again and filled with His Spirit. We walk with God a bit, when suddenly trials and tribulations begin to hit. We begin to suffer losses and learn to live a new kind of life, a divine life where we are forged into the image of Jesus. We go through the fires of refinement, and just when we think it is all done, blow upon blow seem to hit us from every direction, and we wonder why this perceived judgment of God has come.

"It is a fearful thing to fall into the hands of the living God. But recall the former days in which, after you were illuminated, you endured a great struggle with sufferings: partly while you were made a spectacle both by reproaches and tribulations, and partly while you became companions of those who were so treated; for you had compassion on me in my chains, and joyfully accepted the plundering of your goods, knowing that you have a better and an enduring possession for yourselves in heaven. Therefore do not cast away your confidence, which has great reward. For you have need of endurance, so that after you have done the will of God, you may receive the promise." Hebrews 10:31-36

"Though He was a Son, *yet* He learned obedience by the things which He suffered." Hebrews 5: 8

It is only through picking up our cross daily, and following the Lord, do we become beaten gold. Much is written on the refinement process, where gold is placed in the fire to be purified, and the dross removed. The Blacksmith knows that the gold is purified when he can see his reflection in it. The gold is now perfect and ready...for service? No! Ready for the anvil, the high place of sacrifice and death.

There are many cleaned up lumps of gold in the Kingdom of God, who will not submit to the hammer. They refuse to be transformed on the altar of the anvil. Thank God they are in the Kingdom but they are of no practical use to the King. It is *only* after gold has been made pure that it can be first beaten into an unrecognizable shape, flattened out into a thin sheet, and then finally made into a vessel of honour. You cannot enter into your destiny in Christ until you have said, like Job did - "Though he slay me, yet will I trust Him," Job 13:15 and laid your life on the anvil, His will be done in you.

If we are to follow Jesus, we must daily take up our cross and follow Him to the Cross. It is through [12]many tribulations that we enter into the Kingdom of God. We must lay our lives as a living sacrifice upon the anvil of God's Altar ready to die to our lumpy self and be hammered into the golden, glorious image of Jesus! Gold, the coveted King of metals must be hammered and humbled before the King of Creation.

It is one thing to desire to be used of God. It is quite another to be willing to die to self, and be forged finally into a useable vessel. The difference between being a beautiful little lump of gold and a golden vessel that can hold the King's new wine, is the willingness to die to self and willingly face the hammer and anvil.

The Word of God makes it very plain that there are different kinds of vessel in the Kingdom:

"Nevertheless the solid foundation of God stands, having this seal: "The Lord knows those who are His," and, "Let everyone who names the name of Christ depart from iniquity." But in a great house there are not only vessels of gold and silver, but also of wood and clay, some for honour and some for dishonour.. Therefore if anyone cleanses himself from the latter, he will be a vessel for honour, sanctified and useful for the Master, prepared for every good work. 2 Timothy 2:19-21

---

[12] Acts 14:21-22

In Christ, we are precious gold in the eyes of God. Now the choice is ours, whether we want to be a beautiful, refined lump before His throne, or a finished vessel, fit for the Master's use? I know that I want to be a finished vessel, fit for the Master's use!

CHAPTER 3

BATTLE-AXES NEED TO BE SHARPENED

"*You are My battle-ax and weapons of war: For with you I will break the nation in pieces; With you I will destroy kingdoms;* With you I will break in pieces the horse and its rider; With you I will break in pieces the chariot and its rider; With you also I will break in pieces man and woman; With you I will break in pieces old and young; With you I will break in pieces the young man and the maiden; With you also I will break in pieces the shepherd and his flock; With you I will break in pieces the farmer and his yoke of oxen; And with you I will break in pieces governors and rulers. "And I will repay Babylon And all the inhabitants of Chaldea For all the evil they have done In Zion in your sight," says the LORD." Jeremiah 51:20-24 (Italics added)

Today Blacksmiths (Apostles) are the "*revelators*" of God's word who are being used to assist in building the Church of

Christ. They are the end-time Apostles that are being raised up in every nation, proclaiming that we are in the midst of a "*third reformation*" from [13]Martin Luther! They are the ones the Lord is using to help in [14]sharpening and [15]perfecting the saints for the work of the ministry:

I declare to you that in many quarters there are no Blacksmiths (Apostles) who can sharpen the Saints' - God's weapons of warfare. Let us, as we continue our press, stay connected to the Blacksmiths that the Lord has given to us. Remember, [16]the weapons of our warfare are not carnal, but mighty in God to the pulling down of every stronghold, and every high thing that seeks to exalt itself against the knowledge of God. *Remember that the Word of God declares that we [the Saints] are God's battle-axes:*

"*You are My battle-ax and weapons of war*: For with you I will break the nation in pieces; With you I will destroy kingdoms; With you I will break in pieces the horse and its rider; With you I will break in pieces the chariot and its rider; With you also I will break in pieces man and woman; With you I will break in pieces old and young; With you I will break in pieces the young man and the maiden; With you also I will break in pieces the shepherd and his flock; With you I will break in pieces the farmer and his yoke of oxen; And with you I will break in pieces governors and rulers. "And I will repay Babylon And all the inhabitants of Chaldea For all the evil they have done In Zion in your sight," says the LORD." Jeremiah 51:20-24 (Italics added)

Quite apart from working to refine metals and hammering

---

[13] He was the great German priest who began the great reformation in 1500 and began what is called the "Protestant Movement"

[14] Proverbs 27:17

[15] Ephesians 4:11-12

[16] 2 Corinthians 10:3-6

them into shape; Blacksmiths/Apostles are also to sharpen weapons of war for battle.

This is why it is absolutely necessary for Apostles to be accepted by the Body of Christ, and allowed to mature and function so that we can all be helped in being [17]equipped to do the work of the ministry.

[18]Destroying Babylon

Babylon has always sought to come against the things and people of God. In ancient times it moved against the Israelites and destroyed Jerusalem and took the best and brightest of its young citizens from the tribe of Judah to serve its evil schemes. There was a young man named Daniel along with his three friends Hananiah, Mishael, and Azariah that were forced into Babylon. These four young men represented a vision of the end-time Church. They fought against Babylon's system and won.

The Daniel Example

Daniel is a tremendous *apostolic figure* in the scriptures. King Nebuchadnezzar of Babylon, besieged Jerusalem, destroyed it, and took the best and the brightest to influence and strengthen his domain. His kingdom was very expansive; it covered most of the then Middle East. Daniel was taken along with his three friends and incarcerated in Babylon. *He was between the age of 13 - 16 years and the 12 chapters of the book of Daniel span over a 65-year period.* He stood as a strong and influential figure, under four successive kings, and two successive kingdoms, Babylon and Medo-Persia and remained relevant in every change.

Please understand that Daniel was initially trained in Israel. In fact, his formative years had already passed, and Babylon (a type of the religious, political, social, economic system of the

---

[17] Ephesians 4:12

[18] Extract taken from the author's book "Five Pillars of The Apostolic" as he thought it very vital and relevant to this writing

world), wanted to have these boys for its use.

Even though Daniel was *trained in the* [19]*language and literature of Babylon,* it was God who gave him the wisdom to [20]function successfully in Babylon.

> "As for these four young men, God gave *them knowledge and skill in all literature and wisdom*; and Daniel had understanding in all visions and dreams." Daniel 1:17 (Italics added)

> "There is a man in your kingdom in whom is the Spirit of the Holy God. And in the days of your father, light and understanding and wisdom, like the wisdom of the gods, were found in him; and king Nebuchadnezzar your father -your father the king- made him chief of the magicians, astrologers, Chaldeans, and soothsayers. Inasmuch as an excellent spirit, knowledge, understanding, interpreting dreams, solving riddles, and explaining enigmas were found in this Daniel whom the king named Belteshazzar, now let Daniel be called and he will give the interpretation." Daniel 5:11-12 (Emphasis added).

Daniel did not rely upon the "*wisdom*" of the Babylonians to function; he totally relied upon God's wisdom. In fact, it is very interesting to note the issue surrounding Daniel's initial promotion. King Nebuchadnezzar had a dream that he could not remember, let alone have interpreted.

> "Now in the second year of Nebuchadnezzar's reign, Nebuchadnezzar had dreams, and his spirit was so troubled that his sleep left him. Then the king gave the command to call the magicians, the astrologers, the sorcerers, and the Chaldeans to tell the king his dreams. So they

---

[19] Daniel 1:4

[20] Daniel 1:17 & Daniel 5:11

came and stood before the king. And the king said to them, 'I have had a dream, and my spirit is anxious to know the dream.' Then the Chaldeans spoke to the king in Aramaic, 'O king, live forever! Tell your servants the dream, and we will give the interpretation.' The king answered and said to the Chaldeans, 'My decision is firm: If you do not make known the dream to me, and its interpretation, you shall be cut in pieces, and your houses shall be made an ash heap. 'However, if you tell the dream and its interpretation, you shall receive from me gifts, rewards, and great honor. Therefore tell me the dream and its interpretation.' They answered again and said, 'Let the king tell his servants the dream and we will give its interpretation.' The king answered and said, 'know for certain that you would gain time, because you see that my decision is firm: 'If you do not make known the dream to me, there is only one decree for you! For you have agreed to speak lying and corrupt words before me till the time has changed. Therefore tell me the dream, and I shall know that you can give me its interpretation.' The Chaldeans answered the king, and said: 'There is not a man on earth who can tell the king's matter; therefore no king, lord, or ruler has ever asked such things of any magician, astrologer, or Chaldean.'" Daniel 2:1-10

Of course the Lord had set the whole thing up, and there was no one in the demonic realm that could interpret the king's dream. demonic powers and principalities do not have a clue as to what the Lord is doing. They do not posses the wisdom that God has, and it is always sad when the people of God rely on "*earthly wisdom*" to accomplish spiritual things.

As the [21]decree goes out, and all the wise men are being sought after and killed, Daniel steps up and declares Godly wisdom, far beyond anything Babylon had ever seen:

---

[21] Daniel 2:13

"Then with counsel and *wisdom* Daniel answered Arioch, the captain of the king's guard, who had gone out to kill the wise men of Babylon; He answered and said to Arioch the king's captain, 'Why is the decree from the king so urgent?' Then Arioch made the decision known to Daniel. So Daniel went in and asked the king to give him time, that he might tell the king the interpretation. Then Daniel went to his house, and made the decision known to Hananiah, Mishael, and Azariah, his companions, That they might seek mercies from the God of heaven concerning this secret, so that Daniel and his companions might not perish with the rest of the wise men of Babylon. Then the secret was revealed to Daniel in a night vision. So Daniel blessed the God of heaven. Daniel answered and said: 'Blessed be the name of God forever and ever, For *wisdom* and might are His. And He changes the times and the seasons; He removes kings and raises up kings; He gives *wisdom* to the wise and knowledge to those who have understanding. He reveals deep and secret things; He knows what is in the darkness, And light dwells with Him. I thank You and praise You, O God of my fathers; You have given me *wisdom* and might, and have now made known to me what we asked of You, for You have made known to us the king's demand.'" ...Then King Nebuchadnezzar fell on his face, prostrate before Daniel, and commanded that they should present an offering and incense to him. The king answered Daniel, and said, "Truly your God is the God of gods, the Lord of kings, and a revealer of secrets, since you could reveal this secret." *Then the king promoted Daniel and gave him many great gifts; and he made him ruler over the whole province of Babylon, and chief administrator over all the wise men of Babylon.* Also Daniel petitioned the king, and he set Shadrach, Meshach, and Abed-nego over the affairs of the province of Babylon; but Daniel sat in the gate of the king. Daniel 2:14-23; 46-49 (Italics added)

Daniel then goes on to give the dream and its interpretation to king Nebuchadnezzar[22]. It was because this level of *wisdom* did not exist in all the domain of Babylon, that Daniel was promoted. No one possessed it. The strength of the world had no idea what to do. demonic wisdom was useless at this level.

> "Then king Nebuchadnezzar fell on his face, prostrate before Daniel, and commanded that they should present an offering and incense to him. The king answered Daniel, and said, 'Truly your God is the God of gods, the Lord of kings, and a revealer of secrets, since you could reveal this secret.' *Then the king promoted Daniel and gave him many great gifts; and he made him rule over the whole province of Babylon, and chief administrator over all the wise men of Babylon.* Also Daniel petitioned the king and he set Shadrach, Meshach, Abed-Nego over the affairs of the province of Babylon; *but Daniel sat in the gate of the king.*" Daniel 2:46-49 (Italics added)

With the restoration of the Apostles, this is the dimension of *wisdom* that is returning to the Church. This level of *wisdom* is part of the technology that the Lord will use to dismantle and destroy Babylon.

Another dimension of the Spirit of wisdom is for decoding the mysteries of God, bringing illumination to the Church:

> "Therefore I also, after I heard of your faith in the Lord Jesus and your love for all saints, do not cease to give thanks for you, making mention of you in my prayers: that the God of our Lord Jesus Christ, the Father of glory, may give to you *the spirit of wisdom and revelation in the knowledge of Him, the eyes of your understanding being enlightened*; that you may know what is the hope of His calling, what are the riches of the glory of His inheritance

---

[22] Daniel 2:24-45

in the saints, and what is the exceeding greatness of His power toward us who believe, according to the working of His mighty power which He worked in Christ when He raised Him from the dead and seated Him at His right hand in the heavenly places, far above all principality and power and might and dominion, and every name that is named, not only in this age but also in that which is to come. And He put all things under His feet, and gave Him to be head over all things to the church, which is His body, the fullness of Him who fills all in all." Ephesians 1:15-23 (Italics added).

"For this reason I, Paul, the prisoner of Christ Jesus for you Gentiles-if indeed you have heard of the dispensation of the grace of God which was given to me for you, how that *by revelation He made known to me the mystery* (as I have briefly written already, by which, when you read, you may understand my knowledge in the mystery of Christ), which in other ages was not made known to the sons of men, as it has now been *revealed by the Spirit to His holy Apostles and Prophets*: that the Gentiles should be fellow heirs, of the same body, and partakers of His promise in Christ through the gospel, of which I became a minister according to the gift of the grace of God given to me by the effective working of His power. To me, who am less than the least of all the saints, this grace was given that I should preach among the Gentiles the *unsearchable* riches of Christ, *and to make all see* what is the fellowship of *the mystery*, which from the beginning of the ages has been hidden in God who created all things through Jesus Christ; *to the intent that now the manifold wisdom of God might be made known by the Church to the principalities and powers in the heavenly places,* according to the eternal purpose which He accomplished in Christ Jesus our Lord." Ephesians 3:1-11 (Italics added)

There are some tremendous words in this passage of scripture that reveal the heart of God.

Unsearchable
This is the Greek word "anexichniastos" and is rendered "untraceable, past finding out, doesn't leave any footprints". What Paul is actually saying, is that the mystery of God cannot be traced, because God did not leave any footprints. There remains only one way for that level of decoding to operate, and it has to be through the "*Grace Gift*" of Apostles, that God has given. God Himself has to reveal the mystery, otherwise it will not be known. This is why the Apostles must be restored and accepted in the body. God has graced them with the technology to decode the mysteries that are hidden in Christ.

To Make All See
The word "*see*" is the Greek word, "*photizo*" and is rendered "to brighten up, to shine, enlighten, illuminate, bring to or give light, cause to see".

Part of the grace gifting of Apostles, is to cause the saints to see and perceive the mysteries of God.

Manifold
The word manifold is a noteworthy Greek word. It is the word "polupoikilos" which is made of two Greek words "polus" = "much" and "poikilos" = "varied or multicoloured".

This word conveys the meaning that the wisdom of God is much varied and has many dimensions, and shades and colors to it. God is multifaceted and He continues to demonstrate His "*manifold wisdom*" through His Church, and this will increase through the Apostles.

Remember, the Babylonian system still exists in the earth. It is just as alive, just as pernicious, just as expansionist as it was in Daniel's day. Babylon is still seeking a generation that can affect the present and the future.

The word training is also a very interesting Hebrew word. It is the word - *Gadal* - to become strong! To become valuable! To be powerful! It also defines a continuous development process of growth toward greatness.

So in this context, they were to become strong, to be used in the service of Babylon. We have seen this happen, as a lot of bright young Christians have been drawn away over the decades, into the world system, and used to promote its values. They were "trained by Babylon".

We now need to have strong Churches that can rip people out of Babylon and bring them into the Kingdom.

Everything in the world's system is designed to *"train or school"* us to serve it, and to lose sight of the true realm of the Kingdom of God. It is designed to cause us to become ambivalent to Kingdom values and principles.

We are called to live in this world, but not be a part of its system. We have to live right in the mess, and not be contaminated by it. We must live with the wisdom of God, and have an overcoming nature, to be successful in this present world.

This present Babylonian system will fall; it will be destroyed by the Rock cut out the mountain – which represents the Kingdom of God – the Church, the Body of Christ in the earth. We will be used to destroy Babylon. However, this end-time Church must have her Blacksmiths returned and be fully functioning so that we can be prepared to fulfill this awesome task!

"This is the dream. Now we will tell the interpretation of it before the king. You, O king, are a king of kings. For the God of heaven has given you a kingdom, power, strength, and glory; and wherever the children of men dwell, or the beasts of the field and the birds of the heaven, He has given them into your hand, and has made you ruler over them all—you are this head of gold. But after you shall arise another kingdom inferior to yours; then another, a third kingdom of bronze, which shall rule over all the earth. And the fourth kingdom shall be as strong as iron, inasmuch as iron breaks in pieces and shatters everything; and like iron that crushes, that kingdom will break in pieces and crush all the others. Whereas you saw the feet and toes, partly of potter's clay and partly of iron, the kingdom shall be divided; yet the strength of the iron shall be in it, just as you saw the iron mixed with ceramic clay. And as the toes of the feet were partly of iron and partly of clay, so the kingdom shall be partly strong and partly fragile. As you saw iron mixed with ceramic clay, they will mingle with the seed of men; but they will not adhere to one another, just as iron does not mix with clay. And in the days of these kings *the God of heaven will set up a kingdom which shall never be destroyed;* and the kingdom shall not be left to other people; it shall break in pieces and consume all these kingdoms, and it shall stand forever. *Inasmuch as you saw that the stone was cut out of the mountain without hands, and that it broke in pieces the iron, the bronze, the clay, the silver, and the gold—the great God has made known to the king what will come to pass after this. The dream is certain, and its interpretation is sure."* Daniel 2:36-45 (Italics added)

Isn't it interesting that when Babylon falls, in the book of Revelation the Lord calls for the Apostles and prophets to rejoice?

"After these things I saw another angel coming down from heaven, having great authority, and the earth was illuminated with his glory. And he cried mightily with a loud voice, saying, *"Babylon the great is fallen, is fallen,*

*and has become a dwelling place of demons, a prison for
every foul spirit, and a cage for every unclean and hated
bird!* For all the nations have drunk of the wine of the
wrath of her fornication, the kings of the earth have committed fornication with her, and the merchants of the
earth have become rich through the abundance of her
luxury." And I heard another voice from heaven saying,
"Come out of her, my people, lest you share in her sins,
and lest you receive of her plagues. For her sins have
reached to heaven, and God has remembered her iniqui-
ties. *Render to her just as she rendered to you, and repay
her double according to her works*; in the cup which she
has mixed, mix double for her. In the measure that she
glorified herself and lived luxuriously, in the same measure give her torment and sorrow; for she says in her
heart, 'I sit as queen, and am no widow, and will not see
sorrow.' "Therefore her plagues will come in one day—
death and mourning and famine. And she will be utterly
burned with fire, for strong is the Lord God who judges
her. "The kings of the earth who committed fornication
and lived luxuriously with her will weep and lament for
her, when they see the smoke of her burning, standing at
a distance for fear of her torment, saying, 'Alas, alas, *that
great city Babylon, that mighty city! For in one hour
your judgment has come.'* "And the merchants of the
earth will weep and mourn over her, for no one buys their
merchandise anymore: merchandise of gold and silver,
precious stones and pearls, fine linen and purple, silk and
scarlet, every kind of citron wood, every kind of object
of ivory, every kind of object of most precious wood,
bronze, iron, and marble; and cinnamon and incense, fragrant oil and frankincense, wine and oil, fine flour and
wheat, cattle and sheep, horses and chariots, and bodies
and souls of men. The fruit that your soul longed for has
gone from you, and all the things which are rich and
splendid have gone from you, and you shall find them no
more at all. The merchants of these things, who became

rich by her, will stand at a distance for fear of her torment, weeping and wailing, and saying, 'Alas, alas, that
great city that was clothed in fine linen, purple, and scarlet, and adorned with gold and precious stones and
pearls! For in one hour such great riches came to nothing.' Every shipmaster, all who travel by ship, sailors,
and as many as trade on the sea, stood at a distance and
cried out when they saw the smoke of her burning, saying, 'What is like this great city?' "They threw dust on
their heads and cried out, weeping and wailing, and saying, 'Alas, alas, that great city, in which all who had ships
on the sea became rich by her wealth! For in one hour
she is made desolate.' "*Rejoice over her, O heaven, and
you holy apostles and prophets, for God has avenged you
on her!*" Revelation 18:1-20 (Italics added)

However, please understand that the Apostles themselves
must go through the refining and hammering process in order to
be effectively used by God. One cannot claim "apostleship"
without the due process and resulting evidence. In many quarters
some assume that Apostles are the "untouchables" who can
touch everyone and everything and bring them, and it, into align-
ment and shape, without they themselves being touched.

As we read the account in the book of Luke 6:12-20 this
training is evidenced by the actions of Jesus:

"Now it came to pass in those days that He went out to
the mountain to pray, and continued all night in prayer to
God. And when it was day, *He called His disciples to
Himself; and from them He chose twelve whom He also
named apostles*: Simon, whom He also named Peter, and
Andrew his brother; James and John; Philip and
Bartholomew; Matthew and Thomas; James the son of
Alphaeus, and Simon called the Zealot; Judas the son of
James, and Judas Iscariot who also became a traitor. And
He came down with them and stood on a level place *with*

a crowd of His disciples and a great multitude of people from all Judea and Jerusalem, and from the seacoast of Tyre and Sidon, who came to hear Him and be healed of their diseases, as well as those who were tormented with unclean spirits. And they were healed. And the whole multitude sought to touch Him, for power went out from Him and healed them all. *Then He lifted up His eyes toward His disciples, and said...*" (Italics added)

Jesus calls His disciples (Greek word "Mathetes", which is rendered learner, trainee or student) and from them He chooses the twelve who were fully trained, and He conferred upon them, apostleship. He then goes on to direct His entire "Sermon on the Mount" to the other disciples who obviously were still in training. The training process for apostles is very intense as we read in the remaining verses of Luke chapter six. Apostles must walk out the Beatitudes, if they are truly Apostles.

Apostolic Dichotomy
Permit me if you will, to list some of the qualifications, qualities and quintessential signs of an Apostle. I call this the "apostolic dichotomy" (Dichotomy - A division or the process of dividing into two especially mutually exclusive or contradictory groups or entities!)

The Apostle Paul in his epistle to the Corinthians gives some very salient information concerning his apostleship:

"But we have this treasure in earthen vessels, that the *excellence of the power* may be of God and not of us. We are hard pressed on every side, yet not crushed; we are perplexed, but not in despair; persecuted, but not forsaken; struck down, but not destroyed—always carrying about in the body the dying of the Lord Jesus, that the life of Jesus also may be manifested in our body. For we who live are always delivered to death for Jesus' sake, that the life of Jesus also may be manifested in our mortal flesh. So then death is working in us, but life in you. And since we have the same spirit of faith, according to what is written, "I believed and therefore I spoke," we also believe and therefore speak, knowing that He who raised up the Lord Jesus will also raise us up with Jesus, and will present us with you. For all things are for your sakes, that grace, having spread through the many, may cause thanksgiving to abound to the glory of God. Therefore we do not lose heart. Even though our outward man is perishing, yet the inward man is being renewed day by day. For our light affliction, which is but for a moment, is working for us a far more exceeding and eternal weight of glory, while we do not look at the things which are seen, but at the things which are not seen. For the things which are seen are temporary, but the things which are not seen are eternal. 2 Corinthians 4:7-18 (Italics added)

"We then, as workers together with Him also plead with you not to receive the grace of God in vain. For He says: "In an acceptable time I have heard you, And in the day of salvation I have helped you." Behold, now is the accepted time; behold, now is the day of salvation. We give no offense in anything, that our ministry may not be blamed. But in all things we commend ourselves as ministers of God: in much patience, in tribulations, in needs, in distresses, in stripes, in imprisonments, in tumults, in labors, in sleeplessness, in fastings; by purity, by knowledge, by longsuffering, by kindness, by the Holy Spirit, by sincere love, by the word of truth, by the power of God, by the armor of righteousness on the right hand and on the left, by honor and dishonor, by evil report and good report; as deceivers, and yet true; as unknown, and yet well known; as dying, and behold we live; as chastened, and yet not killed; as sorrowful, yet always rejoicing; as poor, yet making many rich; as having nothing, and yet possessing all things. 2 Corinthians 6:1-10

In 2 Corinthians 4: 8 the Apostle Paul describes a dynamic that was at work in him and the other Apostles, which he described as the *Excellence of the Power*! This is what is at work in *"apostolic"* (*Sent*) People!

Excellence – this comes from 2 Greek words:
Huper – Beyond
Ballo – To throw

So in essence it means to Throw Beyond or to Go Beyond. Reaching further than everyone else!

Let Us Look At What This *Excellence* Produces:

1. Hard pressed (troubled, in tribulation, vexed, constant annoyance) on every side, yet not *crushed* (the throng of a multitude on someone). There are times when you are going through the process of being shaped by the Lord, you feel "hard pressed", but the Lord assures us that even though we feel that way, He would not crush us. Glory to God! Listen to the Apostle Paul in the following verses of scripture:

   "For we do not want you to be ignorant, brethren, of our trouble which came to us in Asia: that we were burdened beyond measure, above strength, so that we despaired even of life. Yes, we had the sentence of death in ourselves, that we should not trust in ourselves but in God who raises the dead, who delivered us from so great a death, and does deliver us; in whom we trust that He will still deliver us. 2 Corinthians 1: 8-10

   For indeed, when we came to Macedonia, our flesh had no rest, but we were troubled on every side. Outside were conflicts, inside were fears. Nevertheless God, who comforts the downcast, comforted us by the coming of Titus. 2 Corinthians 7: 5-6

2. Perplexed (aporeo – at a loss for a way or resources, illus-
   trations are in the sense of being at one's wit's end, at a
   loss how to proceed, without resources). But not in
   despair – (exaporeo "to be utterly without a way" "without any hope of getting through"). There are times, when
   what you know you are called to be and do in God, is
   "far" greater than your present resource and you enter
   into times of being *perplexed* – as a matter of fact those
   are the times when you know that the only way forward,
   is to trust in the providence and faithfulness of Almighty
   God; who does not leave us in despair!

3. Persecuted (ekdioko – "to drive out from", to be ostra-
   cized), but not *forsaken* – (to abandon, or to leave in a
   strait without hope of rescue). We live in an age where
   people do not want to be persecuted for the gospel of
   Jesus Christ, but I am here to tell you that it is an integral
   part of the true Believer's life. We will be persecuted if
   we live the way the Lord intended for us to. The devil
   still hates the Believer, and in this hour, the Lord is
   returning Blacksmiths to remind us of this.

   Our peers and contemporaries will persecute us; but
   the Lord will not abandon or orphan us.

4. Struck down – (fix firmly in a fallen place, like an anchor
   on a ship) but not *destroyed* – (apollumi – to lay waste,
   to utterly destroy, disintegrate, complete ruin).   There
   are times in the divine process that the Lord will keep us
   in obscurity as done in [23]wine making, and it is at those
   times the enemy of your soul will seek to destroy you;
   but God will not allow it.

5. Death works in us so that life may work in others – 2
   Corinthians 4: 10-12. Apostles must go through the

---

[23] For greater detail on this you can read "Apostolic Purity" another title by the author
ISBN 1-894928-11-3; ordering details at the end of this book.

process of dying to self. That sentence must be constantly at work on the inside, so that life can flow out of them.

6. Outward man perishes but the inward man is constantly
    being renewed!

7. We do not look in the natural or the flesh in the realm
    where things are seen but we look in the spirit in the
    unseen realm.

2 Corinthians 6: 8-10 – Here are some more dimensions
of this dichotomy or paradox if you will.

8. By Honour and Dishonour

9. By Evil Report and Good Report

10. As Deceivers and yet True

11 As Unknown and yet Well Known

12. As Dying and behold we Live

13. As Chastened and yet Not Killed

14. As Sorrowful yet Always Rejoicing

15. As Poor yet making many Rich

16. As Having Nothing and yet Possessing All Things

There is a *power* that is at work not only in the apostle but in
every Blood-washed, Spirit-filled Child of God! I would like to
remind us of this. Let us identify and effectively articulate this
awesome fact!

First, let us look at the word *power* in the Greek! There are about six different words in Greek for our one English word *power*! However, the two most commonly used are:

Exousia denoting authority and Dunamis (doo'-nam-is); from where we get our English word *dynamite* and this is the one that is used in both passages of scripture that we have just read and it means - force (literally or figuratively); specially, miraculous power (usually by implication, a miracle itself): ability, abundance, meaning, might (-ily, -y, -y deed), (worker of) miracle (-s), power, strength, violence, mighty (wonderful) work.

This miraculous, powerful, mighty, strong, ability that is in us is constantly doing several things that we need to be confidently aware of:

1. It is strengthening us with might in the inner man – 2 Corinthians 4:16, Colossians 1: 9-12

2. Causes Christ (the Anointing) to dwell in our hearts through faith – Galatians 2:20

3. Causes us to be rooted and grounded in love. *Sometimes it takes the dunamis of God to love some people but we know that we can because this power is constantly at work in us.*

4. Causes us to comprehend the width, length, depth and height of the love of Christ. This is so awesome as the *Love* of Christ encompasses everything and everyone – Job describes it this way – Job 11: 6-9 "That He would show you the secrets of wisdom! For they would double your prudence. Know therefore that God exacts from you Less than your iniquity deserves. "Can you search out the deep things of God? Can you find out the limits of the Almighty? They are higher than heaven—what can you do? Deeper than Sheol—what can you know? Their measure is longer than the earth And broader than

the sea." The "breadth" implies Christ's worldwide love, embracing all men; the "length," its extension through all ages (Ephesians 3:21); the "depth," its profound wisdom, which no creature can fathom (Romans 11:33); the "height," its being beyond the reach of any foe to deprive us of it (Ephesians 4:8)

5. Causes us to be filled with all the *fullness of God*! – This is just plain *awesome*! The word *fullness* conveys a very powerful meaning and we should make an effort to understand it. Fullness in the Greek is *"Pleroma"* and is translated – *full number, full complement, full measure and that which is complete.* This word describes a ship with a full cargo and crew, or a town or city with no empty houses. It also describes the time when Jesus was to be born and there was no room in the inn because it was "pleroma". - This word strongly emphasizes *fullness* and *completion*! Here are some examples of its usage:

Ephesians 1:10 – "that in the dispensation of the *fullness* of the times He might gather together in one all things in Christ, both which are in heaven and which are on earth—in Him." (Italics added)

Ephesians 4:13 – "And He Himself gave some to be *apostles*, some prophets, some evangelists, and some pastors and teachers, for the equipping of the saints for the work of ministry, for the edifying of the body of Christ, *till we all come to* the unity of the faith and of the knowledge of the Son of God, to a perfect man, to the measure of the stature of *the fullness of Christ*;" (Italics added)

Galatians 4:4 – "But when the *fullness* of the time had come, God sent forth His Son, born of a woman, born under the law, to redeem those who were under the law, that we might receive the adoption as sons.

(Italics added) There is a pleroma of time in every situation

Colossians 2:9 – "For in Him dwells all the *fullness* of the Godhead bodily; and you are complete in Him, who is the head of all principality and power." (Italics added)

It doesn't matter what you are facing at this time, there is a *"pleroma"* of time in it and when that time comes, no one can stop the plan of God! Remember the children of Israel in Egypt and in Babylon – when the *Pleroma* of time came, Pharaoh had to deliver them – Babylon had to deliver them.

All this is at *Work* in us because of the Dunamis of God!

Work – This comes from a Greek word "Ergon" and denotes an active engagement in an exercise. Activity is taking place on the inside of us that requires effort, and the Holy Spirit is supplying it. *He is working in us!* He is bringing us forth as a vessel worthy for the Master's use. The Saints are being perfected and the Blacksmiths (*Apostles*) have their role to play in this process.

Another Dimension Of The Apostles' Process

[24]In the new apostolic arising, we often hear of the increased momentum of Apostles emerging in diversity of expression; some in a greater measure demonstrating the present dimension of the Kingdom with signs and wonders, while others are more particularly graced to teach and to impart with strong governmental anointing. We also hear too, of Apostles now leading the way for the corporate Christ (the Saints) to enter a new dynamic and dimension of destiny, with Apostles being recognized in virtually every major stream of the marketplace. From Hollywood to "The Hood," Apostles are coming forth in an

---

[24] Adapted from a writing of Tim Early of Foundations of Apostles and Prophets and used by permission.

accelerated thrust, for the reshaping of the Church into the accurate patterns of corporate destiny, transitioning mentalities from Church to Kingdom, into the present administration of Christ's triumphal reign. In such promised order, we affirm that present truth Apostles bring to the table so-to-speak, the very plan of God for the ages, as *wise master builders*, (*Blacksmiths*) reconstructing the present position of the Church into the ongoing and progressive rhythm and revelation, that the corporate body is the habitation of God.

True, there is a valid expression, ministry, and dimension of grace allotted to those whom the Lord calls, anoints, and appoints to apostleship. However, bear in mind; that being an Apostle is not in the anointing and presence that comes when one is being affirmed as an Apostle, or in the establishing of their second or third assembly.

For beneath all of the so-called fanfare of many, exclaiming that Apostles are most important in the overall scheme of things, or in covertly suggesting that apostles are a cut above the rest, the truth is, Apostles are still everyday people. For one thing, Apostles suffer, experience pain, and are very misunderstood at times; especially when pioneering revelation.

Apostles are not guaranteed an easy ride, nor should they expect one. True, they can learn from the mistakes and misfortunes of others, and glean the hidden wisdom of their own personal tests. But Apostles are not designed to simply avoid every (so-called) negative instance in their life, nor is it to be assumed that every negative (apparent) happening is not of God. Unfortunately, many have assumed that Apostles are immune to hurt, criticism, suffering, and rejection. But there is no golden rule or blanket statement which defines Apostles as androids or something of which, cannot be touched with the feeling of infirmities.

Truthfully, much of the persecution, which accompanies the calling, is not only from within the parameters of the cosmos or world system, but from the Church itself. For in First John 2, those that left from among the corporate anointing, are defined as antichrists, (or those that possess the Pharisee or religious spirit), which is the number one enemy to Apostles, just as Jezebel is the chief enemy to the prophets. Yes beloved, the enemy we are speaking of here is not a political leader in some foreign land, or the conjecture of your favourite Christian movie. Rather, the junk we entertain above our nose and between our ears is the real man of sin in the temple – Greek "naos", which is used to also describe our bodies as the Temple of the Lord.

"Little children, it is the last hour; *and as you have heard that the Antichrist is coming, even now many antichrists have come, by which we know that it is the last hour. They went out from us, but they were not of us; for if they had been of us, they would have continued with us; but they went out that they might be made manifest, that none of them were of us.* But you have an anointing from the Holy One, and you know all things. I have not written to you because you do not know the truth, but because you know it, and that no lie is of the truth. Who is a liar but he who denies that Jesus is the Christ? He is antichrist who denies the Father and the Son. Whoever denies the Son does not have the Father either; he who acknowledges the Son has the Father also." 1 John 2:18-23 (Italics added)

Furthermore, Apostles recognize the antichrist mentality, for it is a lawless nature that is not submitted to true authority in the Kingdom. The antichrist mentality that John's epistles speak of, denies the faith, denies the Father and Son (and true father son relationships), thus, despising the unity of the Father and Son as Jesus confirms in the true model prayer (not Matthew 6 which is the disciples' or our prayer) of John 17:21, "Father make them *one* as we are one... that the world would know..."

So, when you think about it, Apostles have challenges and confrontations too, but should not wear their emotions on their shoulders like a car with a flat tire slowly driving on the shoulder of the road. Apostles do not give audience to the voices of this present age, nor do they turn in the towel after experiencing what seem to be unfortunate situations. But one thing is for certain. Present-truth Apostles continue to reaffirm Christ and His finished work. They activate the saints to the reality of justification to glorification, from sin to *Son*, from conception to perfection, and the cross to the throne. Present truth pioneering Apostles forge ahead regardless of the persecution, and are not recorded scripturally, to whine, pout, nor to call it quits.

Just the same, Apostles will be open to others either to share their tender heart, or for appointed others to pour into them. True Apostles will never assume that they are beyond counsel or prayer. For the key to their authority in the corporate body is not in their authority itself, but in the mutual relationships they are established in, and the delicate fruit which they bear.

The Making Of Apostles:

According to the scriptures, Abraham was *made* a father of many nations, a father of a multitude. How? Through the developmental process of being made. Yes beloved, he was a *made* man, even as Jacob was created, but Israel was formed. For Abram was not to fulfill the promise, but Abraham was. No, not Sari, but Sarah. For a name denotes a nature, and more than we care to admit, the inner workings and dealings of the Lord will lead to an outworking of *His* Manifest Presence, not merely to get busy to do lots of things, but to *become new things in Him.*

The same was with Ezekiel, a priest who became a prophet who, out of the vision of the Lord in Ezekiel chapter one, beholds a man, a wheel within a wheel, a people within a people, a nation within a nation, and a man within the making of the man. For out of all the fire and unfolding events of the vision, there emerges a man, a four-faced ministry, four, being the number of the earth, complete in HIM from all points or corners thereof.

The Word of God declares the following, which some Apostles do not like to hear, but none the less is very true:

"For I think that God has displayed us, the apostles, last, as men condemned to death; for we have been *made* a spectacle to the world, both to angels and to men. We are fools for Christ's sake, but you are wise in Christ! We are weak, but you are strong! You are distinguished, but we are dishonoured! To the present hour we both hunger and thirst, and we are poorly clothed, and beaten, and homeless. And we labour, working with our own hands. Being reviled, we bless; being persecuted, we *endure*; being defamed, we entreat [or pray]. We have been *made* as the filth of the world, the offscouring [brushed all around, off-scrapings] of all things until now. 1 Corinthians 4:9-13 (Italics and Parenthesis added)

Welcome to the life of an Apostle! It is one thing to be "apostolic-like", but it is another thing to be *apostolic life*. Many saints want to be Christ-like, but there is a dimension of the Spirit to be [25]*Christ-Life*.

True, all Apostles experience differing degrees of tests, making and shaking, sifting and shifting; but never underestimate the character development for each. Whether one was threatened with death, placed into prison for life, or is experiencing bad health, just remember, a test yields a testimony, and in your worse mess there is a message. For it is simply a test of the emergency broadcasting system. Smile, for God the Father has just what you need, to manifest the fullness of *His* glory through you. He has picked us out to be picked on, as fruit from the tree. Like John the revelator, a man sentenced to a slow death, the

---

[25] 2 Timothy 1:10; John 1:4; Romans 5:17

Lord used the opportunity of Patmos to squeeze every bit of juice needed from him. For you can eat ten apples in a row and come up with a bloated stomach, or you can get the essence thereof by juicing it; and beloved, that is what the Lord is doing with his Apostles.

In Isaiah 46:11, He is squeezing us into shape, through a press (or process), through something narrow, even that which vexes. Yes beloved, "Purpose" here is "Yatsar," God is dealing with us, and it is useless to attempt to circumvent the process, or to short-change it through complaining, yelling, and temper tantrums. Go ahead, give it your best shot, but there is an appointment of the Lord, the day of the oven, where every man is tried and roasted with fire.

"We give no offence in anything, that our ministry may not be blamed. *But in all things* we commend ourselves as ministers of God: in *much patience*, in tribulations, in needs, in distresses, in stripes, in imprisonments, in tumults, in labours, in sleeplessness, in fastings; by purity, by knowledge, by longsuffering, by kindness, by the Holy Spirit, by sincere love, by the word of truth, by the power of God, by the armour of righteousness on the right hand and on the left, by honour and dishonour, by evil report and good report; as deceivers, and yet true; as unknown, and yet well known; as dying, and behold we live; as chastened, and yet not killed; as sorrowful, yet always rejoicing; as poor, *yet making many rich*; as having nothing, and yet possessing all things." 2 Corinthians 6:3-10

This is an awesome scriptural reference concerning Apostles and their signs. It begs the question – What is the first sign of an Apostle? Well some may say the ability to plant and govern churches; or wisdom or miracles, signs and wonders and the list can go on. However, the Word of God declares that *character and lifestyle are the first signs of true apostleship.*

Once again, welcome to the life of an Apostle. It is more than having your presence seen and heard in the annual conference, and much more than having fifty ministry sons to follow you around the world. It has nothing to do with how important you think you are, but everything to do with the Fatherhood of God, and the buffeting, chastening, scourging, disciplining, and correction of the Lord, to bring His true Apostles into a place of total obedience.

And beloved, how do Apostles learn obedience? Through the principle of Jesus, the pattern (model or prototype) Son, who learned obedience through the things He suffered or endured. How do Apostles learn and value patience, which is the first characteristic and sign of apostleship in 2 Corinthians 12:12? Through tribulation, for in Romans 5:3-5, "Tribulation works patience, and patience experience, and experience hope, and hope makes not ashamed." Somebody once said that hope to them is to never have to experience another tough test or trial again – humour. Yes beloved, in being esteemed as present truth Apostles, what is it producing?

Will Apostles or those who assume the role become largely defined for their dynamics, or do we accept them in the deeper aspects of their call, too, which is more manhood than ministry? - Jesus' manhood was for thirty years, and ministry three and a half years. Knowing full well that Apostles suffer in a variety of degrees, and are pioneering ministries with front-line confrontation, we should look at some of the characteristics and preparations of Apostles from a practical application. Bear in mind though, that there is a new level of understanding of the Apostle through the Melchisedec order, whereas many that you'd thought would never qualify from your practical knowledge, are actually walking therein, as Enoch, the seventh from Adam, who fully pleased God; for he was, then he was not, for he was translated.

There are massive dimensions and floodgates of the Spirit that are not word for word, but Spirit to Spirit, for in this dimension, spirit gives birth to spirit (John 3:6-7). Yes beloved, there is a hidden company of Apostles from the Melchisedec order and apostolic priesthood that may never be defined by the ecclesiastics as becoming Apostles, but defined in the third dimension above the mercy seat between the cherubim, no longer the glory of man in the outer court, but the radiant glory of the Lord in the most holy place. And as soon as we catch this in Spirit, we will birth it through Spirit.

Here, we will acknowledge men and women in apostleship, and eliminate the line of demarcation of the controlling religious systems. We will value the emerging apostolic priesthood of all Believers, apostolic in scope, character, nature, spirit, and dimension. Here, we would grasp the greater glory of the Lord for apostolic infusion throughout the entire earth, as the Lord brings to a screeching halt the frivolous notion and ideal that only America believes itself to be the founding forefathers of the new apostolic reformation. Nonsense, for this new apostolic reformation is global in its scope and operations!

Practical Characteristics And Preparation Of Apostles

Apostles possess the qualities of [26]elders. They are noted in the areas of moral character, domestic, spiritual, and ministry capacity.

[27]Apostles are people of humility. They do not walk in vain or self-glory.

Apostles will have a serving heart. (Heart of a servant – Jesus, the Apostle came to serve). The Apostle Paul gave a fitting description of this in the opening verse of his letter to the Roman believers:

"Paul, a bondservant of Jesus Christ, called to be an apostle, separated to the gospel of God..." Romans 1:1

---

[26] 1 Timothy 3:1-9, Acts 20:28, 1 Peter 5:1-2.

[27] 1 Corinthians 4:9; Philippians 2:5; Acts 20:19; Proverbs 15:33

Apostles will have much patience as recorded in 2 Corinthians 12:12, as part of the apostolic criterion:

"Truly the signs of an apostle were accomplished among you with all perseverance, in signs and wonders and mighty deeds."

Apostles will maintain [28]scriptural integrity, rightly handling the word of truth. (The word and the Spirit in oneness, the proceeding word, the quickening nature of the Spirit, not letter, law, legalism, bondage, or the fruit of King Saul).

Apostles will be seasoned in [29]leadership and testimony. Does not have a need to be needed.

Apostles, through reciprocation and mutually appointed relationships will walk in a fresh dimension of spiritual authority. Their ministry is service instead of authority driven, even though perceived in greater grace for spiritual authority.

Apostles will have the heart of a father and will admonish.[30]

Apostles will have a deeply committed love, loyalty, and respect for the church of the Lord Jesus Christ, characterized by unselfishness, with more [31]love for the corporate body at large, than his own ministry. Their motivation and driving mechanism is the body, the church and the maturing of the saints.

Ministry Of An Apostle
Apostles are given for the founding and establishing of the church on a proper and strong foundation. They are the wise master builders of 1 Corinthians 3:9-14; Ephesians 2:20-22...

---

[28] Titus 2:1; 2 Timothy 2:15
[29] 2 Corinthians 6:3-10, 1 Corinthians 4:9-13
[30] 1 Corinthians 4:15, Philippians 2:22
[31] 1 Corinthians 13

For anyone can start a church, but it takes Apostles to establish them on a sure foundation.[32]

Apostles have a world or global vision for the whole body of Christ[33].

Apostles are given in the Spirit, to scriptural clarity (2 Timothy 3:16) and "This is that... Acts 2:42 (Present Truth...2 Peter 1:12)

Apostles are involved in church discipline and apostolic judgment. They do not have leadership and authority in all assemblies, but is limited. Acts 5:1-11; 1 Corinthians 5

Apostles are given to preach and teach the Word. A different dimension of grace and anointing to preach and teach is upon Apostles. For according to John 7:16, Jesus did not preach His own doctrine, but of Him that apostello (sent) Him. Meaning, when Apostles speak, it launches the mentality of the saints into a whole new frequency for Kingdom advancement. For shepherds tend to the needs of the flock, but Apostles speak into the destiny dimension of the Saints. One will leave the ninety-nine for the one lost sheep, but the other has a larger vision, and more expanded vision, to continue in progressive momentum with the corporate saints. And yes, it is true; one can have an overlapping of Apostle pastoral ministry, and must exercise wisdom in both apostolic and pastoral grace. Just the same, the Lord will be to, and through you, whatever He needs to be.

Apostles are given for the preparation and placement of other elders in the corporate body. From messages, reports, to instructions and travel, it is always relationship based... 2 Timothy 2:2; Acts 16:1-4; 13:5; Philippians 2:19-25

---

[32] 2 Timothy 2:19, Ezra 6:3, 14, Isaiah 28:16
[33] Acts 1:8, Ephesians 1:17-18, Isaiah 14:26-27, Acts 10

Apostles' ministry involves the signs thereof. But keep in mind, many Apostles function largely out of the divine revelation and foundation and teaching aspects of ministry, and are never to be placed in a box. Some leaders feel that unless an Apostle's meeting involves altar calls and miracles each night, he or she is to be discounted for his or her apostleship. Not so. For there is a lesser and higher anointing, and the measure of rule principle as well. What many saints need right now is more teaching, training, developing, and activation, although the Holy Spirit can flow freely as He wills. In the divine order of the church (1 Corinthians 12:28), God has set in *His Body* first Apostles, prophets, teachers, and then miracles, for signs here follow the word. It is not to suggest that no signs will ever flow without the proclaimed and explained Word, but it does bring value to both the revelation of the Word, coupled with the manifestation of the Spirit. For if there is the revelation, there is to be evident manifestation. 2 Corinthians 10:12-18; 12:12

Apostles are given to the body for the affirming and ordination of elders and deacons. Licensing was not a part of the apostolic church, but ordination/affirmation is. Eldership is primarily a ruling function (still a servant of the Lord), and deacon is definitely a serving function. Deacons do not rule in the church. Acts 6:1-6; 14:23; 1Timothy 3

Apostles are given at large to recognize, raise, and to release seasoned, trained, fruitful, mature, and valid ministry in the corporate Body of Christ. This is not to be associated with the traditional wineskins of old order denominationalism. For in the apostolic dimension, the recognizing, raising, and releasing involves to some degree a prophetic vision, prophetic perception, with apostolic mentality to help stir and provoke the leadership into the eternal purpose for which it is given. It is characterized in a different frequency of the Spirit. Colossians 4:7-12; Titus 1:5-7... The Apostolic and prophetic brings into view the Kingdom, apostolic globalization, reformation, present truth, and the destiny of the Saints. This is the difference between the old mentality of raising up missionaries, to the transitioning new order of advancing the Kingdom through global apostolic mentality, apostolic acquisition, and apostolic spheres of influence throughout the nations. Here, it is the great commission versus the great commotion, Bethel versus Babel.

Apostles are given to impart fatherhood and apostolic wisdom, bringing the stability of the Kingdom into a present position impartation, and not a one man preaching paradigm; for many can preach it, but few can impart it. This principle is connected to the Ancient of Days, the wool hair of the Lord, a word for the Church and the times that we are living in, and the mandated authority of the Spirit to take the Saints into the appointed times of the Lord, beyond the mathematical charts and calculations of un-illuminated men... Proverbs 1:7; 2:10-11; 3:13; 4:7; 9:1; 24:2-3; 2 Peter 3:15-16; 1 John 2:13-14 (little children, young men, fathers)...it is a return to the Ancient paths, where there is a good way, finding rest for our souls... Jeremiah 6:16 (largely pioneered through present truth fathers of the Spirit)

Apostles are given by the Lord to set His house in Order... 1 Corinthians 7:17; 11:34; 16:1-2

The ministry of Apostles is given to the supernatural dimension of signs, wonders, miracles, and mighty deeds. Whether the manifestation of the gifts of the Spirit, the laying on of hands, the activation of Saints in receiving the baptism of the Holy Spirit, or revelation knowledge, an Apostle's function may vary, in greater degrees for one and lesser degrees for another. For embedded in the original pattern and order of apostles in the book of Acts are miracles, encapsulated within the very nature of what Apostles are given for. In the earth today, a number of Apostles are experiencing miracles in the realm of the dead being raised to life and creative miracles where limbs and organs appear. This is why it is important for Apostles to define the higher anointing in their life, and the greater or lesser grace the Lord will use them in. More importantly, Apostles must remain yielded to the Holy Spirit in any way HE desires to flow through them. That way, they will not become familiar to their own strengths and weaknesses like Samson did, shaking himself as other times if the occasion would merit - too late of course! 1 Timothy 4:14; Romans 1:11; Acts 19:1-6; 1 Corinthians 1:7; 2 Timothy 1:6

Benefits Of Having Apostles In The Corporate Life Of The Assembly

In all of the developmental process stages of apostolic growth, there is the sifting of the true Apostle from the false, and the mature Apostle from the novice. For *immaturity is not necessarily impurity; and all novices are not to be classified as false.* However, never take the position that an Apostle is a come-easy ministry, with a few well-placed connections to guarantee their success, or enough administrative ability to be qualified as an Apostle. For I would go as far as to say, that most that claim apostleship, are in fact not, and when you think about it, the price for the prize and the process for the purpose is not something all named Apostles care to admit. *Therefore, we must humble ourselves to the call* (and the One who called us, the Lord), *and to the delicate and developing process from manhood to ministry, instead of being pre-occupied with being used in great ministry.*

If you are an Apostle, and are called to pioneer a new destiny among the Saints, don't let it get to your head. Rather, let it all go to your *Sovereign Head* (Ephesians 4:15), and let Christ magnify Himself through you. No Apostle is an Apostle because of *mere self-election.* No present truth Apostle is going to wear it as a title or security blanket. No present truth Apostle is going to demand to be served.

As opposed to barging your way into local assemblies and insisting on folk calling you the chief Apostle, become a servant, and learn to differentiate divine inspiration versus human aspiration. If the calling is there, then that is the first stage. For it take seasons (sometimes years) to develop fruit, although the revelation of the call can sometimes come in an instance.

Apostles benefit the assemblies through apostolic revelation. Galatians 1:12; 2 Corinthians 12:1-4; Ephesians 3:3; Romans 16:25

Apostles benefit you by strengthening the assemblies. Romans 16:25; Acts 14:22; Acts 15:41; 18:23

Apostles benefit the assemblies by establishing proper and strong foundation. 2 Peter 1:12; 1 Corinthians 3:10; Ezra 6:3, 11

Apostles (with the co-labour of the prophets) benefit the assemblies by restoring them to God's original purpose and plan for planet earth, stirring the saints towards the fuller expression of becoming the image of God in the earth, the Incarnate Word. Isaiah 9:7; Isaiah 14:26; Genesis 1:26-28; Psalms 21:1; Matthew 6:10

Remember to *"feed the seed"* and to *"nurture the nature"*, for you are becoming what you already are, enlightened and empowered to the done deal, the finished work of the cross.

As I conclude this chapter, there is something I would like to bring to light, within this whole apostolic restoration. As with every move of God, there will be inaccuracies and excesses, and it is no different with the present reformation, where we are seeing the restoration of Apostles to the Body of Christ. There are some who are seeking to take the Apostolic into dimensions never intended by the Holy Spirit and as such, will be in need of adjustments. Some are trying to become *"Super Apostles"* and be in charge of the entire Body of Christ (similar to what happened with the Roman Catholic Church, with an infallible pope at its helm). Some are even declaring that Apostles are the best thing since "sliced bread" and as such should be given "carte blanche"; this is erroneous. Apostles are a part in an ongoing process, which will result in a *Mature, Perfect Church* in the earth.

While Apostles are first in terms of rank, time and importance (especially in assisting with establishing the Kingdom in individual lives, regions, local churches, etc) there is also a dimension to which they are last (in terms of restoration, given that prophets, evangelists, pastors and teachers were restored before). I believe that this was done, so that the dimension of the apostolic of *coming alongside to help* might be made manifest. I also believe that this is what the Apostle Paul was saying when he declared this to the Corinthians: 2 Corinthians 1:24

"Not that we have dominion over your faith, but are fellow workers for your joy; for by faith you stand."

"Not for that we have dominion over your faith, but are helpers of your joy: for by faith ye stand." KJV

This is one of the powerful dimensions of the apostolic in these days; the ability to come alongside those that have already been restored, and to help them in fully coming forth into their destiny. You see, there is a dimension of the prophetic, evangelistic, pastoral and teaching that absolutely needs the apostolic, for it to remain relevant and vibrant; so if Apostles do not see this, then these other ministry gifts will suffer. So it is absolutely necessary for Apostles to work alongside the other Five-Fold Ministry gifts, to the benefit of all.

I have been having this vision of a *"new structure"* of church leadership being an upside down pyramid - where the point which is now at the bottom represents the Word of God, and as we move away from the point, we have the Apostles and prophets, as we move away from there we have the evangelists, pastors and teachers, and from there we have elders and deacons, from there we have administrators. helps, etc and then on the top we have *the Saints*!

The Lord has been speaking this to me for quite a while, that everything is being done *so that His* saints (the Church) not the usual *"man and woman"* of God, including the present day

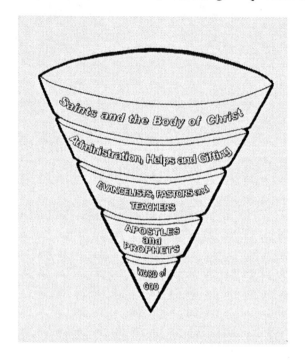

Apostle, can be made visible. For we will all have to come to the place of being known as *Saints - Sons and Daughters of God.*

CHAPTER 4

PLOWSHARES TURNING INTO SWORDS

"**P**roclaim this among the nations: "Prepare for war! Wake up the mighty men, Let all the men of war draw near, Let them come up. *Beat your plowshares into swords And your pruning hooks into spears*; Let the weak say, 'I am strong.'" Joel 3:9-10 (Italics added)

This passage of scripture is a prophetic picture of the Church of Jesus Christ in the last days. A proclamation goes forth that we are to prepare for war. Instructions come commanding us to *"beat our plowshares into swords and our pruning hooks into spears."*

Plowshares and pruning hooks were tools used in the farming trade. Plowshares were used to till the ground in preparation for the sowing of seed and pruning hooks were used to trim the dead branches of the grape vine in preparation for its next season of production.

When the Church was birthed in the "Upper Room" on the Day of Pentecost as recorded in the book of Acts chapter two; the Prophet Joel was quoted by Apostle Peter in declaring that the recipients of the "baptism of the Holy Spirit" were not drunk with wine, but were fulfilling the prophecy spoken by Joel. H e declared "This is that which was spoken by the Prophet Joel."

In light of this, it would augur well if we were to return to the book of Joel and decode some of the mysteries that are in that book.

In chapter two the Lord declares by the Prophet Joel that He was going to pour out His Spirit upon all flesh:

"And it shall come to pass afterward That I will pour out My Spirit on all flesh; Your sons and your daughters shall prophesy, Your old men shall dream dreams, Your young men shall see visions. And also on My menservants and on My maidservants I will pour out My Spirit in those days. Joel 2:28-29

Joel is describing some of the events of the New Testament Church which we would not have known about, if the Apostle Peter did not rise up and decode the events of Pentecost. In like manner, I declare to you that the Lord has called His Church to beat their plowshares into swords, and pruning hooks into spears. This is very interesting and important, as plowshares and pruning hooks were made out of metal, and the transformation of these into swords and spears is the job of the Blacksmith - Hallelujah!

The question can be asked – "How can we, the New Testament Church, accomplish this?" Well, once again we need to revisit the passage of scripture in the book of Joel:

"Proclaim this among the nations: "Prepare for war! Wake up the mighty men, Let all the men of war draw near, Let them come up. Beat your plowshares into swords And your pruning hooks into spears; Let the weak say, 'I am strong.' "Assemble and come, all you nations, And gather together all around. Cause Your mighty ones to go down there, O LORD. "Let the nations be wakened, and come up to *the Valley of Jehoshaphat*; For there I will sit to judge all the sur-rounding nations." Joel 3:9-12 (Italics added)

The Valley Of Jehoshaphat

This was a very significant place of battle for the people of God under King Jehoshaphat, from which some very insightful principles can be drawn. King Jehoshaphat was faced with an invading army comprising of the Moabites, the Ammonites and the people of Mount Seir, making the odds seem heavily in favour of the enemy. Faced with insuperable odds, he decided to seek the Lord, and the strategy the Lord gives him was astounding:

"Then the Spirit of the LORD came upon Jahaziel the son of Zechariah, the son of Benaiah, the son of Jeiel, the son of Mattaniah, a Levite of the sons of Asaph, in the midst of the assembly. And he said, "Listen, all you of Judah and you inhabitants of Jerusalem, and you, King Jehoshaphat! Thus says the LORD to you: 'Do not be afraid nor dismayed because of this great multitude, for the battle is not yours, but God's. Tomorrow go down against them. They will surely come up by the Ascent of Ziz, and you will find them at the end of the brook before the Wilderness of Jeruel. You will not need to fight in this battle. Position yourselves, stand still and see the salvation of the LORD, who is with you, O Judah and Jerusalem!' Do not fear or be dismayed; tomorrow go out against them, for the LORD is with you." And Jehoshaphat bowed his head with his face to the ground, and all Judah and the inhabitants of Jerusalem bowed before the LORD, worshiping the LORD. Then the Levites of the children of the Kohathites and of the children of the Korahites stood up to praise the LORD God of Israel with voices loud and high. So they rose early in the morning and went out into the Wilderness of Tekoa; and as they went out, Jehoshaphat stood and said, "Hear me, O Judah and you inhabitants of Jerusalem: Believe in the LORD your God, and you shall be established; believe His prophets, and you shall prosper." *And when he had consulted with the people, he appointed those who should sing to the LORD, and who should praise the beauty of holiness, as they went out before the army* and were saying: "Praise the LORD, For His mercy endures forever." *Now when they began to sing and to praise, the LORD set ambushes against the people of Ammon, Moab, and Mount Seir, who had come against Judah; and they were defeated."* 2 Chronicles 20:14-22 (Italics added)

A fast was proclaimed, and as they sought the face of Almighty God; the Spirit of the LORD came upon Jahaziel the son of Zechariah, the son of Benaiah, the son of Jeiel, the son of Mattaniah, a Levite of *the sons of Asaph*, in the midst of the assembly. This Jahaziel has roots that go back to Asaph – a praise and worship leader who was a very significant figure in King David's reign, as we will see later on. He prophesied that the people of God did not need to fight in the battle; all they had to do was to position themselves and they would see the Salvation of the Lord.

King Jehoshaphat then came into an awesome revelation, and decoded what the Word of the Lord meant that was spoken through Jahaziel. He established the fact, that true establishment and prosperity comes from a firm belief in the Lord and in His ordained prophets. The Bible says, he then set out a battle plan that was strange to say the least; he sent out Judah – the praise and worship team in front of the army. No matter how we slice that up, those were strange orders. To begin with, Jahaziel did not prophesy that Judah should go first, and secondly they were to "*stand still*" and see the Salvation of God.

Send Judah First

This was the [34]apostolic dimension in King Jehoshaphat, manifesting itself; and just like the Apostle Peter on the Day of Pentecost, he was able to decode the events of the day. Here we see the king decoding the Word of the Lord and taking necessary and prescribed action. This also reminds us of the Apostle Peter, when Jesus had asked His disciples, "Who do men say that I, the Son of Man, am?" and he received the revelation that Jesus was the Christ, the Son of the Living God.

As a matter of fact, King Jehoshaphat tapped right into the heart of God and decoded this mystery. In Hosea we see that same revelation being echoed:

"Ephraim is a trained heifer That loves to thresh grain; But I harnessed her fair neck, I will make Ephraim pull a plow. *Judah shall plow*; Jacob shall break his clods." Hosea 10:11 (Italics added)

Plowing is the first thing that is done in farming; you cannot sow seed before you plow. Judah – praise and worship - is to go first. Praise and worship then, is our plowshare and we are commanded to beat our plowshares into swords. We can only do that effectively through the ministry of God's Blacksmiths, the Apostles. It is through the revelation that is released through His Holy Apostles, that we can accomplish this. That is why we read in the following text that Apostles are first:

"And God has appointed these in the church: *first apostles*, second prophets, third teachers, after that miracles, then gifts of healings, helps, administrations, varieties of tongues." 1 Corinthians 12:28 (Italics added)

When Moses was sending in the spies to spy out the land of Canaan, Joshua and Caleb were among them and they were the

---

[34] For more on this dimension please see the author's book Five Pillars Of The Apostolic.

only ones to bring back a good report. It is no coincidence that Joshua came form the tribe of Ephraim, which means *"Doubly Fruitful"* and Caleb from the tribe of Judah, which we have already established, means *Praise.*

The Apostles Paul and Silas, two of the Lord's Blacksmiths applied this same revelation when they were in prison:

"And when they had laid many stripes on them, they threw them into prison, commanding the jailer to keep them securely. Having received such a charge, he put them into the inner prison and fastened their feet in the stocks. *But at midnight Paul and Silas were praying and singing hymns to God,* and the prisoners were listening to them. Suddenly there was a great earthquake, so that the foundations of the prison were shaken; and immediately all the doors were opened and everyone's chains were loosed. And the keeper of the prison, awaking from sleep and seeing the prison doors open, supposing the prisoners had fled, drew his sword and was about to kill himself. But Paul called with a loud voice, saying, "Do yourself no harm, for we are all here." Then he called for a light, ran in, and fell down trembling before Paul and Silas. And he brought them out and said, *"Sirs, what must I do to be saved?"* So they said, "Believe on the Lord Jesus Christ, and you will be saved, you and your household." *Then they spoke the word of the Lord to him and to all who were in his house. And he took them the same hour of the night and washed their stripes. And immediately he and all his family were baptized.* Now when he had brought them into his house, he set food before them; and he rejoiced, having believed in God with all his household." Acts 16:23-34 (Italics added)

They were thrown into prison because they cast out a devil from a damsel, and recognized the gravity of their situation as they found themselves chained in the inner prison (KJV). At midnight they applied the revelation of sending Judah first and the results were awesome; not only were they miraculously set free, but their praise and worship *"plowed"* the ground for the sowing of God's Word, resulting in the jailer and his entire household being saved.

Much has been spoken about the Tabernacle of David being restored in these last days and rightly so, as it carries with it substantial evidence of the power of sending Judah first and the dynamic release that comes from that.

Understanding The Davidic Spirit

"After this I will return And *will rebuild the tabernacle of David*, which has fallen down; I will rebuild its ruins, And I will set it up; So that the rest of mankind may seek the LORD, Even all the Gentiles who are called by My name, Says the LORD who does all these things." Acts 15:15-17 (Italics added)

"On that day *I will raise up The tabernacle of David*, which has fallen down, And repair its damages; I will raise up its ruins, And rebuild it as in the days of old; That they may possess the remnant of Edom, And all the Gentiles who are called by My name," Says the LORD who does this thing." Amos 9:10-12 (Italics added)

In order for us to fully appreciate the Tabernacle of David and its importance, we need to revisit the life of King David and extract some pertinent principles and download them into our operating systems.

In 1 Chronicles 13, David, after his appointment as king over all Israel, seeks to bring the Lord's Presence back to Israel. However, he goes about it the wrong way.

"Then David consulted with the captains of thousands and hundreds, and with every leader. And David said to all the assembly of Israel, "If it seems good to you, and if it is of the LORD our God, let us send out to our brethren everywhere who are left in all the land of Israel, and with them to the priests and Levites who are in their cities and their common-lands, that they may gather together to us; and *let us bring the ark of our God back to us*, for we have not inquired at it since the days of Saul." Then all the assembly said that they would do so, for the thing was right in the eyes of all the people. So David gathered all Israel together, from Shihor in Egypt to as far as the entrance of Hamath, to bring the ark of God from Kirjath Jearim. And David and all Israel went up to Baalah, to Kirjath Jearim, which belonged to Judah, to bring up from there the ark of God the LORD, who dwells between the cherubim, where His name is proclaimed. *So they carried the ark of God on a new cart from the house of Abinadab, and Uzza and Ahio drove the cart.* Then David and all Israel played music before God with all their might, with singing, on harps, on stringed instruments, on tambourines, on cymbals, and with trumpets. And when they came to Chidon's thresh-ing floor, Uzza put out his hand to hold the ark, for the oxen stumbled. Then the anger of the LORD was aroused against Uzza, and He struck him because he put his hand to the ark; and he died there before God. And David became angry because of the LORD's outbreak against Uzza; therefore that place is called Perez Uzza to this day. David was afraid of God that day, saying, "How can I bring the ark of God to me?" So David would not move the ark with him into the City of David, but took it aside into the house of Obed-Edom the Gittite. The ark of God remained with the family of Obed-Edom in his house three months. And the LORD blessed the house of Obed-Edom and all that he had." (Italics added)

They built a *new cart, hitched it up to some oxen* (a type of the flesh or beast nature) and gave Uzza (strength) and Ahio (his brother) to drive the cart. That was a representation of *man's best effort with the flesh nature – beast!* The Lord intervenes and kills Uzza, as he tries in his own strength to save the Ark of God. David became angry – and this is what happens each time we try to bring forth the purpose of God in the flesh, and by our own strength – and the Ark was turned aside into the house of Obed-Edom.

David then finds out the due process for [35]transporting the Ark and implements it:

1 Chronicles 15:1-2
"David built houses for himself in the City of David; and he prepared a place for the ark of God, and pitched a tent for it. Then David said, *"No one may carry the ark of God but the Levites, for the LORD has chosen them to carry the ark of God and to minister before Him forever."* (Italics added)

1 Chronicles 15:11-15
"And *David called for Zadok and Abiathar the priests, and for the Levites*: for Uriel, Asaiah, Joel, Shemaiah, Eliel, and Amminadab. He said to them, *"You are the heads of the fathers' houses of the Levites*; sanctify your-selves, you and your brethren, that you may bring up the ark of the LORD God of Israel to the place I have pre-pared for it. For because you did not do it the first time, the LORD our God broke out against us, because we did not consult Him about the proper order." *So the priests and the Levites sanctified themselves to bring up the ark of the LORD God of Israel.* And the children of *the Levites bore the ark of God on their shoulders, by its poles, as Moses had commanded according to the word of the LORD.* (Italics added)

---

[35] Numbers 3: 5-10 and Numbers 4: 5-16

David learnt that the *"Due or Set Order"* for transporting the Ark, was on the shoulders of the priests.

Key Verse: 1 Chronicles 15:13 *"*For because you did not do it the first time, the Lord our God broke out against us*, because we did not consult Him about the proper order."* (Italics added)

However, David, as he establishes God's *"New Move"*, contradicts some of the Old Mosaic regulations. He places the Ark in an open tent and surrounds it with continuous praise and worship and music. This was never done before, since the Ark was housed in the Holy of Holies with access only to the High Priest.

This is awesome and holds true, every time the Lord seeks to take His Church up another level; there will be the breaking of tradition, to the dismay of some. It was true in David's time as his wife Michal; Saul's (*previous order*) daughter despised him for the *"New Move"* he was leading:

> "Then David returned to bless his household. And Michal the daughter of Saul came out to meet David, and said, "How glorious was the king of Israel today, uncovering himself today in the eyes of the maids of his servants, as one of the base fellows shamelessly uncovers himself! So David said to Michal, "It was before the LORD, who chose me instead of your father and all his house, to appoint me ruler over the people of the LORD, over Israel. Therefore I will play music before the LORD. And I will be even more undignified than this, and will be humble in my own sight. But as for the maidservants of whom you have spoken, by them I will be held in honour." Therefore Michal the daughter of Saul had no children to the day of her death. 2 Samuel 6:20-23

Jesus experienced similar apprehensions when He came to establish the New Testament; the Scribes and Pharisees had serious problems with the way He did things. When the Lord began reforming His Church after she fell into apostasy, there were problems for every reformer beginning with Martin Luther, and continues to this day. Under the Prophetic Restoration, we had Jezebel (*a spirit of manipulation and control* that moves in both male and female that tries to control the Reformer). Now under the apostolic restoration we have the "Pharisee spirit" (a powerful religious spirit that gets its strength from religious tradition, legalism and bondage; this is the same spirit that manifested itself in Jesus' day and the days of the Early Church), rising up to contend for legitimacy and rule.

Please understand that with every "*New Move*" of God's Spirit there will be things that will be used from the previous move; but there will also be those of the previous move that will be left behind. Jesus said it this way:

"Then He said to them, "Therefore every scribe instructed concerning the kingdom of heaven is like a householder who brings out of his treasure *things new and old.*" Matthew 13:52 (Italics added)

David went on to establish the "*New Move*" of God and he set certain principles in motion that caused great freedom and release for the people. As a matter of fact, David went on to become the yardstick by which every other king was judged. Jesus was even known as "The Son of David".

1 Chronicles 15:16, 25-29
"Then David spoke to the leaders of the Levites to appoint their brethren to be the singers accompanied by instruments of music, stringed instruments, harps, and cymbals, by raising the voice with resounding joy... So David, the elders of Israel, and the captains over thousands went to bring up the ark of the covenant of the LORD from the house of Obed-Edom with joy. And so it was, when God helped the Levites who bore the ark of the covenant of the LORD, that they offered seven bulls

and seven rams. David was clothed with a robe of fine linen, as were all the Levites who bore the ark, the singers, and Chenaniah the music master with the singers. David also wore a linen ephod. Thus all Israel brought up the ark of the covenant of the LORD with shouting and with the sound of the horn, with trumpets and with cymbals, making music with stringed instruments and harps. And it happened, as the ark of the covenant of the LORD came to the City of David, that Michal, Saul's daughter, looked through a window and saw King David whirling and playing music; and she despised him in her heart.

Here, David, in contradiction to the [36]Mosaic regulations, establishes by the power of revelation, a new and revolutionary order for encounter with God. *He places the ark* (representing the manifest presence of God) *in an open tent and surrounds it with continuous praise, worship and music.*

This was similar to [37]Jesus' powerful entry into Jerusalem; when He fulfilled the prophetic word spoken in Zechariah 9:9-10; tremendous warfare results from this level of praise as was indicated in Jesus' entry into Jerusalem:

"Rejoice greatly, O daughter of Zion! Shout, O daughter of Jerusalem! Behold, your King is coming to you; He is just and having salvation, Lowly and riding on a donkey, A colt, the foal of a donkey. I will cut off the chariot from Ephraim And the horse from Jerusalem; The battle bow shall be cut off. He shall speak peace to the nations; His dominion shall be 'from sea to sea, And from the River to the ends of the earth.'

The Cost Of Worship: There is a cost involved in bringing forth the plan and purpose of the Lord. As we continue in this

---

[36] Exodus 26: 31-35 and Exodus 40: 16-33

[37] Matthew 21: 1-16

hour of apostolic reformation, we will see an increased awareness of three forerunners to Jesus. They will all be in the calibre
of Anna in Luke 2:36-38

> "Now there was one, Anna, a prophetess, the daughter of
> Phanuel, of the tribe of Asher. She was of a great age, and
> had lived with a husband seven years from her virginity;
> and this woman was a widow of about eighty-four years,
> who did not depart from the temple, but served God with
> fastings and prayers night and day. And coming in that
> instant she gave thanks to the Lord, and spoke of Him to
> all those who looked for redemption in Jerusalem."

Anna was an extreme worshipper. The Bible says that she
was married at a tender age, and when her husband died after
seven years of marriage, she did not remarry, but devoted all her
time to the Lord in worship, fasting and prayer. She represented
a type of activity that preceded the first coming of Jesus, in a
similar vein to that of John the Baptist. This is the same kind of
activity that will precede His second coming.

There are three types of *forerunners* to Jesus: Anna - The
Warring Intercessor

Mary - [38]The Extravagant Worshipper

John - [39]The Intense Prophetic Proclaimer/Preacher

All three types entered into *fasting*, hence the power in their
ministries. I believe that this dimension is returning to the Body
of Christ. Now please understand – *not everyone will be called
to this dimension.* This type of fasting is different to the periodic fasting that every believer should do, this is a lifestyle, and it
is a calling.

The Lord was able to use David in establishing this *"New*

---

[38] Mark 14:3-9 Luke 7:36-50
[39] Matthew 3:4; 11:18

Move" because he understood the value and importance of praise and worship, being an intense worshipper. There are some note-worthy points in the way David did things.

1. **This is the system that birthed** the great praise and worship songs of the Psalms. The Psalms were in many cases, spontaneous prophetic songs birthed in the presence of the ark in David's Tabernacle. (The Ark represents the Presence of the Lord)

2. **There is deliberate order and vision in setting -1 Chronicles 15:16-22.** The various ranks of singers and musicians with defined prophetic flows. In other words spiritual liberty is produced out of divine order. Heman, Asaph and Ethan (Jeduthun) were the major worship leaders. Chenaniah was the instructor of the music because he was skilful; so that vision was imparted and deliberately taught to produce David's vision for worship at the Ark.

3. **After the organization was determined, the spirit and "flavour" of the worship and praise, was set in motion by David himself – 1 Chronicles 16: 7-36** David first delivered a psalm into the hand of Asaph. David set the tone for worship at the Tabernacle. He had the revelation and vision of what God wanted. His great worship ministers were talented, spiritual and gifted men, but they flowed in the spiritual principle set by David. (Psalm 105 and 96; Also remember Bezalel - Exodus 31: 2-6) – Where is your heart? Is it involved and connected to the vision?

4. **There is indication of specialized prophetic flows - 1 Chronicles 25: 1-8** Here it gives further detail and insight into the setting up and structure of a worship system. Asaph prophesied according to the order of the king (Asaph's psalms sound very much like David's);

Jeduthun specialized in the use of a harp in giving thanks and praise; Heman was a seer in the words of the Lord and used a horn to stir his anointing. Each of these men had people under them who flowed in the same spirit as they did, but they themselves were under the authority or flow of David himself (1 Chronicles 25:6)

5. **There was instruction given - 1 Chronicles 25: 7** Skill is imparted and deliberate processes are put in *place* to produce a predetermined musical, spiritual and prophetic flow.

6. **There was timetabling and rostering for duty - 1 Chronicles 25: 8-31** In other words there was time for preparation. You knew well in advance when you were roster-ed for service.

There is a reason for this kind of praise and worship, which is identified with the *"Davidic Spirit"*. The Lord proclaimed through the mouths of His prophets that He will restore this kind of worship in the last days:

"And with this the words of the prophets agree, just as it is written: After this I will return And will rebuild the tabernacle of David, which has fallen down; I will rebuild its ruins..." Acts 15:15-16

"On that day I will raise up The tabernacle of David, which has fallen down, And repair its damages; I will raise up its ruins, And rebuild it ..." Amos 9:11

The Worship Service Has To Be A Progression:
In this season of apostolic reformation, we are beginning to understand that our worship has to be a progression or a corporate spiritual journey, from the earth realm or earth sphere, through the spiritual dimensions, to the throne of God or the Holy of Holies.

The terminology is not as important as the spiritual reality, that at the end of a time of singing and worship, the corporate assembly must together touch God each time it goes out in the spirit realm. We corporately begin on the earth, and end in the presence of God. This releases the Voice of God in revelatory preaching, prophesy, healing etc. God is felt and perceived to be manifestly in the midst. The sense of migration through a spiritual experience must not be compromised. We are told in the Psalms that God inhabits, dwells, takes up residence, and comes to live in the praises of His people: "But You are holy, Enthroned in the praises of Israel." Psalms 22:3

This is the real reason for worship and praise; we are to be engaged in sensible, spiritual activity as the Apostle Paul encourages in:

"What is the conclusion then? *I will pray with the spirit, and I will also pray with the understanding. I will sing with the spirit, and I will also sing with the understanding.*" 1 Corinthians 14:15 (Italics added)

We have established the fact that, Plowshares are our praise and worship, and the scripture declares that we are to beat our Plowshares into swords, or weapons of warfare. However, there is a reason for us doing that, and I believe that the Lord wants us to war and fight for territory. The Church of Jesus Christ must rise up to her predetermined destiny and position of ruling among the nations.

Within the last decade, the Church has been hearing quite a lot about warfare, and the Lord's desire to make us warriors. Even within this current *"apostolic reformation"* we are still hearing about this dimension, hence the reason for the title of this book *"Return of The Blacksmiths – The Equipping Dimension of The Apostolic"*. These Blacksmiths/Apostles are to sharpen the saints so that we can continue the warfare with greater efficiency. The Word of God declares:

"If the axe is dull, And one does not sharpen the edge, Then he must use more strength; *But wisdom brings success."* Ecclesiastes 10:9-10 (Italics added)

However, there will come a time, and I believe that it is not too far away, when the Lord will call for us to turn our swords back into plowshares and our spears back into pruning hooks, as will be seen in the next chapter.

Fortress
church.

CHAPTER 5

THE FORTRESS CHURCH

While teaching this message to the saints at Dominion-Life International one Sunday morning one of our youth, by an illustration of art, revealed his understanding of this Church. He drew a *"many membered man"* clothed in armour and ready for battle.

Allow me to share with you a portion of what the Lord had me minister to our local church. However, before we go into the depths of what He has been speaking to me, I would like to share one of the foundational dimensions of any strong, fortress church, and that is *"Divine Order"*.

Please understand that God's Kingdom is built on *"Divine Order"*. As we look at the natural order, birds and butterflies fly, the sun shines, day and night appear without effort, the seasons change invariably. There is freedom, as life flows. However, beneath all of what we see, beneath all that freedom, is what can be described as *"Divine Order"*. There is foundation and structure invisibly lying beneath all that manifest freedom. Read Job 38

"Then the LORD answered Job out of the whirlwind, and said: "Who is this who darkens counsel By words without knowledge? Now prepare yourself like a man; I will question you, and you shall answer Me. "Where were you when I laid the foundations of the earth? Tell Me, if you have understanding. Who determined its measurements? Surely you know! Or who stretched the line upon it? To what were its foundations fastened? Or who laid its cornerstone, When the morning stars sang together, And all the sons of God shouted for joy? "Or who shut in the sea with doors, When it burst forth and issued from the womb; When I made the clouds its garment, And thick darkness its swaddling band; When I fixed My limit for it, And set bars and doors; When I said, 'This far you may come, but no farther, And here your proud waves must stop!'" Job 38:1-11

Kingdom Life is a deliberate lifestyle. Things must be built according to plan. Jesus had disciples who He taught to walk a particular way. They understood that *freedom had foundation.* Jesus was the "freest" man upon the face of the earth and He did nothing apart from what He saw His Father do.

Part of the mandate given to Apostles in this hour is to reveal the wisdom in divine order. They are to assist in bringing the Church into a place where the Lord can truly express His Lordship, causing the earth to be filled with the knowledge of His Glory.

In like manner, in this local house, we want that "*invisible presence" called "divine order"* to operate as we conduct our lives.

Today we want to describe ourselves as a "*Fortress Church*". We want to define ourselves as the "*Church Model*" that was found at Antioch in the book of Acts:

"Now in the church that was at Antioch there were certain prophets and teachers: Barnabas, Simeon who was called Niger, Lucius of Cyrene, Manaen who had been brought up with Herod the tetrarch, and Saul. As they ministered to the Lord and fasted, the Holy Spirit said, "Now separate to Me Barnabas and Saul for the work to which I have called them." Then, having fasted and prayed, and laid hands on them, they sent them away." Acts 13:1-3

The Antioch *"Church Model"* is the closest that we can come to a working model of the *"Fortress Church"*. As we read through the book of Acts there are several things that are unique about this church, some of which are:

- A *multi-ethnic* Church as you had several different people groups in it

- It was a *multi-cultural* Church

- A place where both the rich and poor, educated and uneducated built strong bonds of fellowship

- A governmental Church with Apostles, prophets, evangelists, pastors and teachers functioning out of it

- A praying and fasting Church

- A Spirit-Filled and Spirit-Led Church

- It was at Antioch that they were first called [40]Christians – making them a prototype Church!

- A Resource Centre and a strong base of ministry

- It was from Antioch that Apostles Paul and Barnabas went

---

[40] Acts 11:26

out and came back and reported all that the Lord had done

- The place where the prototype of true apostolic ministry was uncovered – Apostles *need* a local home base. That is why some modern day apostles are getting misled and deceived as they feel they have outgrown the local church and become a law unto themselves and miss their ultimate purpose in God. That is part of the inaccuracy we are seeing in some apostolic people. I have heard of men and women of God resigning from their churches and not being attached to any specific local church declaring that they are Apostles, and need to fulfill their mandate of *"fathering"* the churches. This is an error, since Apostles *need* the local church!

- A Church that was used to settle arguments and problems that arose in other churches and regions, for example, the whole issue of Gentile Christians having to be circumcised by the Jerusalem Church, was settled by Apostles Paul and Barnabas traveling from the Antioch Church to Jerusalem, and giving the grace and wisdom that the Lord had given them among the Gentiles, and as such they were no longer required to be circumcised.

In essence, Antioch was a *"Fortress Church"*! Antioch was a *"Divine Stronghold"*! Oh yes, do you think it was the devil who originally established strongholds? No, he is a copycat and a weak one at that.

In a *"Fortress Church"*, there is what can be best described as *"Divine Connections,"* which are very vital; connections that have the same spiritual frequency or DNA (*Divine Nature Adapted*) as we do. It will be from these kinds of connections that we will be able to invade territories and regions in order to advance the Lord's Kingdom in those places.

An example of one such connection can be seen in what we refer to as the *"Cornelius Connection"* found in Acts 10:

"There was a certain man in Caesarea called Cornelius, a centurion of what was called the Italian Regiment, a devout man and one who feared God with all his household, who gave alms generously to the people, and prayed to God always. About the ninth hour of the day he saw clearly in a vision an angel of God coming in and saying to him, "Cornelius!" And when he observed him, he was afraid, and said, "What is it, lord?" So he said to him, "Your prayers and your alms have come up for a memorial before God. Now send men to Joppa, and send for Simon whose surname is Peter. He is lodging with Simon, a tanner, whose house is by the sea. He will tell you what you must do." And when the angel who spoke to him had departed, Cornelius called two of his household servants and a devout soldier from among those who waited on him continually. So when he had explained all these things to them, he sent them to Joppa. The next day, as they went on their journey and drew near the city, Peter went up on the housetop to pray, about the sixth hour. Then he became very hungry and wanted to eat; but while they made ready, he fell into a trance and saw heaven opened and an object like a great sheet bound at the four corners, descending to him and let down to the earth. In it were all kinds of four-footed animals of the earth, wild beasts, creeping things, and birds of the air. And a voice came to him, "Rise, Peter; kill and eat." But Peter said, "Not so, Lord! For I have never eaten anything common or unclean." And a voice spoke to him again the second time, "What God has cleansed you must not call common." This was done three times. And the object was taken up into heaven again. Now while Peter wondered within himself what this vision which he had seen meant, behold, the men who had been sent from Cornelius had made inquiry for Simon's house, and stood before the gate. And they called and asked whether Simon, whose surname was Peter, was lodging there. While Peter thought about the vision, the Spirit said to him, "Behold, three men are seeking you. Arise therefore, go down and go with them, doubting nothing; for I have sent them." Then Peter went down to the men who had been sent to him from Cornelius, and said, "Yes, I am he whom you seek. For what reason have you come?" And they said, "Cornelius the centurion, a just man, one who fears God and has a good reputation among all the nation of the Jews, was divinely instructed by a holy angel to summon you to his house, and to hear words from you." Then he invited them in and lodged them. On the next day Peter went away with them, and some brethren from Joppa accompanied him. And the following day they entered Caesarea. Now Cornelius was waiting for them, and had called together his relatives and close friends. As Peter was coming in, Cornelius met him and fell down at his feet and worshiped him. But Peter lifted him up, saying, "Stand up; I myself am also a man." And as he talked with him, he went in and found many who had come together. Then he said to them, "You know how unlawful it is for a Jewish man to keep company with or go to one of another nation. But God has shown me that I should not call any man common or unclean. Therefore I came without objection as soon as I was sent for. I ask, then, for what reason have you sent for me?" So Cornelius said, "Four days ago I was fasting until this hour; and at the ninth hour I prayed in my house, and behold, a man stood before me in bright clothing, and said, 'Cornelius, your prayer has been heard, and your alms are remembered in the sight of God. Send therefore to Joppa and call Simon here, whose surname is Peter. He is lodging in the house of Simon, a tanner, by the sea. When he comes, he will speak to you.' "So I sent to you immediately, and you have done well to come. Now therefore, we are all present before God, to hear all the things commanded you by God." Then Peter opened his mouth and said: "In truth I perceive that God shows no partiality. But in every nation whoever fears Him and works righteousness is accepted by Him. The word which God sent to the children of Israel, preaching peace through Jesus Christ—He is Lord of all—that word you know, which was proclaimed throughout all Judea, and began from Galilee after the baptism which John preached: how God anointed Jesus of Nazareth with the Holy Spirit and with power, who went about doing good and healing all who were oppressed by the devil, for God was with Him. And we are witnesses of all things which He did both in the land of the Jews and in Jerusalem, whom they killed by hanging on a tree. Him God raised up on the third day, and showed Him openly, not to all the people, but to witnesses chosen before by God, even to us who ate and drank with Him after He arose from the dead. And He commanded us to preach to the people, and to testify that it is He who was ordained by God to be Judge of the living and the dead. To Him all the prophets witness that, through His name, whoever believes in Him will receive remission of sins." While Peter was still speaking these words, the Holy Spirit fell upon all those who heard the word. And those of the circumcision who believed were astonished, as many as came with Peter, because the gift of the Holy Spirit had been poured out on the Gentiles also. For they heard them speak with tongues and magnify God. Then Peter answered, Can anyone forbid water, that these should not be baptized who have received the Holy Spirit just as we have?" And he commanded them to be baptized in the name of the Lord. Then they asked him to stay a few days."

This is an interesting and incredible account of a "*Divine Connection*", from which the following can be gleaned:

1. Cornelius is a Gentile who is not "saved" in the traditional sense of salvation, of repentance and water baptism.

2.   Peter is a saved Jew who has problems living out his conviction among the Gentiles when he is around his Jewish people. He was not yet delivered from some of his baggage.

3. Phillip the Evangelist was not too far away from Cornelius; as a matter of fact he just came out of an incredible event himself. [41]He was involved in an awesome evangelistic meeting in Samaria, in which Simon the sorcerer was dealt with, and he was then whisked away to deal with the Ethiopian eunuch from Candace's court. After baptizing the man, the Bible records that Phillip was caught away by the Holy Spirit and was found some fifty miles or eighty kilometres away in Azotus. *Incredible!* He then preached until he reached Caesarea, the place where Cornelius was living.

4. You'd think that the Lord would have used Phillip, seeing that he was an evangelist, the only one named in the New Testament, and he was also in the same town as did Cornelius – But *no*! He wanted to deal with an awesome *"Divine Connection"* that would pave the way for future breakthrough for the Church in that region. Peter was some fifty-eight kilometres away!

5. In Acts 7 Stephen is stoned to death in front of Saul. Saul is on a crusade to kill as many Believers as he possibly can – persecution for the Church in Jerusalem, and they are scattered – Saul is on his way to Damascus, gets converted, and the Lord sets up another *"Divine Connection"* between Saul and Ananias that would propel Saul into his apostolic call and ministry to the Gentiles! *Awesome, for he was a Jew.*

6.   Please understand this – Caesarea, the place where

---

[41] Acts chapter 8

Cornelius was living, was a place where there was a huge mixed population of Jews and Gentiles. Not only that, but when Saul began to minister in Jerusalem and contended with the Hellenists, they attempted to kill him, and the first place they took him to escape that attempt was - you guessed it - *Caesarea the place where Cornelius was living! Awesome!* The Lord had set up a prototype for Paul's ministry by using the apostle who was a Jew, who had an apostolic call to the Jews, to minister to a Gentile, in the city where a Jew who had a mandate to kill Christians, would be converted and given an apostolic call to minister to the Gentiles and be a place of safe refuge for him, in the course of fulfilling that mandate. *Incredible! Simply Incredible!*

"And when Saul had come to Jerusalem, *he tried to join the disciples; but they were all afraid of him, and did not believe that he was a disciple. But Barnabas took him and brought him to the apostles.* And he declared to them how he had seen the Lord on the road, and that He had spoken to him, and how he had preached boldly at Damascus in the name of Jesus. So he was with them at Jerusalem, coming in and going out. *And he spoke boldly in the name of the Lord Jesus and disputed against the Hellenists, but they attempted to kill him. When the brethren found out, they brought him down to Caesarea and sent him out to Tarsus."* Acts 9:26-30 (Italics added)

We too have experienced some "*Divine Connections,*" which I would like to share with you. If we are to truly fulfill our mandate from the Lord in being a "*Fortress Church*", we will need to have these connections.

However, before going into the details of some of those "*Divine Connections*" allow me to share a few life-changing incidents I experienced.

Born and raised in a family that was religious, but as it turned out did not really know Jesus, I grew up knowing a bit about the Bible but not knowing the Lord of the Bible. I remember one day, (I was about 19 years at the time), as I went to take a short nap after being exhausted from doing some chores, as I closed my eyes I saw this huge book coming down through the sky surrounded by brilliant rays of golden light. To me it looked as if it was coming out of a *"time tunnel"* for want of a better expression. As the book got closer, I saw these huge words *"HOLY BIBLE"* written in gold, in front of it. I took a hold of this book, and I awoke. Within one year of that encounter, I was returning home from a night out with friends (it must have been around 2:00 AM), and as I walked the streets to my home I found myself crying and asking the Creator of the heavens and the earth, if He was real to make Himself known to me. I went home but could not sleep and the next morning I awoke a changed man. Later on I went and publicly surrendered my life to Jesus in a local church not too far from where I lived.

With my new found peace and joy I decided to share this experience with my family. It was only at that point did I realize that my father and grandmother weren't all that they seemed to be. My father threatened to kill me if I ever tried to *"witness"* to him again. I left his house vowing never to return. The Lord then gave me several visions, one of which sticks out in my mind; in this vision I was being *"caught up"* into the heavens and as I arrived I saw a huge throne and Someone was seated on it. Although I could not make out a face, I knew it was the Lord, and as I drew near to Him, He began speaking to me declaring that the time for me to come and be with Him had not yet come and I was to go back into the earth and accomplish these tasks for Him. After receiving these instructions I was transported into this huge orchard full of trees and neatly trimmed grass.

Not too long after that encounter the Lord did something incredible in our family, and here are some of the details.

In 1985 or thereabout, the Lord used me to minister to my

mother (at that time my father and grand mother were still sore with me) and she gave her life to Jesus. Later on that year or the following, I awoke early to pray and study as was my custom, and around 4:30 AM my wife Sandra came to me and shared a vision that she just had. In this vision we were out of town and when we returned several persons along the way kept telling us that one of my sisters was looking for me. Eventually in the vision we got to our pastor and he said to us *"your sister is look-ing for you as your mother has died"*. This was a Friday morn-ing, and as soon as my wife told me this vision I knew that my mom was going to die; I immediately got into my car and drove to my mother's house, and I as was driving the Lord said to me "I want you to go and say to your mother, all the sins that you have committed they are now remitted and I the Lord am calling you home into life." When I arrived at my mother's home, it must have been around 5:30 AM, my father was lying in bed with my mother, and I went to my mother's side and said exact-ly what the Lord had spoken to me. She looked at me and smiled, she kissed me and I hugged and kissed her. My father did not speak to me; probably he may have been asleep or so I thought. I then left and went back home.

The following day, as it turned out, Sandra and I had a min-istry engagement in another part of the city. As we were return-ing home from that engagement yes you guessed it; several per-sons met us along the way and informed us that my sister was looking for me. Eventually we got to our pastor to debrief him on the ministry assignment, at which time he informed us that my mother had died. This incident stirred something in my father and grandmother and I used the opportunity to once again minister to my family, but my father still resisted me. As it turned out he was involved in some strange religious practice and tried to involve his first born son, who rejected it. I remem-ber ministering to my elder brother for about seven straight weeks, until he finally decided to give his life to Jesus. He is still serving the Lord and very active and vibrant in winning souls to the Lord in the nation of Venezuela.

During the next few years I tried on several occasions to minister to my father, but he rejected the gospel. In 1993 my father took ill and was admitted to hospital, but by the time I heard about it he was discharged. One Sunday as we were returning from service I felt burdened to visit him the following day; however, Sandra encouraged me not to delay and urged me to go him at once. After dropping my family home I immediately visited my father and once again shared the gospel with him. The difference this time was he said to me "Michael I now know what you have been telling me is the truth"; he then lifted up his hands and cried out "Lord have mercy on my soul, Lord have mercy on my soul." Two hours after leaving my father, he was dead.

The Lord continues to astound us with His dealings as we journey with Him, fulfilling what He has mandated us to do. Here are some of our *"Divine Encounters."*

Our Divine Connections:

It was the year 1988 while I was driving my family home from work and school when we came to a stop at a major intersection. At that stop I heard the Lord speak to me and said "Son I will take you out of your native land (Trinidad & Tobago at that time) and I will send you into another land to minister for me". I turned to my wife, Sandra and said to her "Honey, the Lord just spoke to me and said…" however, before I could reveal what He said to me, she quickly replied, "No let me first share with you what the Lord just spoke to me." I allowed her, and she shared with me the exact same thing the Lord had said to me. My response was "this is incredible". On our arrival home that evening we shared our experience with a couple (Edward & Marvery Hosford) who were like mentors to us at that time, and they told us not to worry, the Lord will bring His Word to pass in His timing.

What happened during the next few years was amazing. In 1990 I began reading a book authored by Bishop Bill Hamon titled "The Eternal Church", which echoed some of the truths the Holy Spirit had revealed to me. Around the same time I learnt that he was coming to our nation to be the main speaker at a conference hosted by a man named Dr. Noel Woodroffe, and he turned out to be a truly "divine connection". The Lord prompted me to contact this man and as I did, he encouraged (rather I should say commanded) me, to attend the conference after we spoke.

Later that year, we began a church at our home named *"Fruit of the Spirit Ministries"* and while I was pastoring that church, we attended yet another conference, and the Lord began to speak to us again. While worshipping at the Prophetic/Apostolic Conference in April 1992, the Lord said to me *"close the church and go and support this man of God, Dr. Noel Woodroffe"*, who was and still is leading a local church called Elijah Centre. At that point I turned to my wife Sandra and told her what the Lord had just spoken to me and she responded to me "I know that the Lord speaks to you, so you should do what He has said." We went home that night and prayed about it.

During the same conference, the very next day, the Lord confirmed His word again when two prophets picked us out of a room full of people and began to speak the Word of the Lord to us. As the prophets began speaking the word of the Lord, we listened in awe, as these men of God spoke. The first one to prophesy over us said, "…I really sense that there are some decisions before the two of you right now, that is directly before you and God says I am going to give you the answer. Do not worry about it. I am going to shut down one area so that you will know exactly that this is the way and the will and the plan and the heart of God…"

Then came the second prophet to lay hands on us; he came with the Word of the Lord also saying, *"…And I sense that there has been a burden upon you all concerning direction. It is like you are standing at a fork in the road, God! Where to go? God! What to do? And God says that is not how you are going to make it. Do not be all burdened down. You say, God, You are going to take us in the right way. You just keep on skipping along and I am going to take you in the right way. The steps of a good man are ordered of the Lord and My Spirit is going to order every one of your steps..."*

That was the confirmation we were looking for, to make the decision to close down our Fruit of the Spirit Ministry and go support this other man of God. Well, we did obey the Word of the Lord and today we thank Him for stirring us to be obedient.

We spent five years in this ministry and God did many things while we were there. The teachings of God were very profound, challenging, life changing and Spirit led. Many more Prophetic/Apostolic conferences were held in the land and around the Caribbean region. In one of those regional conferences, a word was spoken over us that accentuated the plan, purpose and direction of the Lord for our lives, and brought back memories of the Word He spoke to us that eventual day while waiting at a major intersection *"And the Lord says, Daughter I have called you even into some strange places and I have even spoken some strange things for you to do but you have held back a little bit in some areas. But then you were obedient and followed through and you saw the Hand of God moved. And I am going to take you even into some more strange places and I am going to take you even into some more strange people and I am going to bring you among some people that are different from you. They are real different from you, but I am going to give you favour among them and you are going to be able to minister unto them and they are going to receive from you, and you are going to see a great move of God among this group of people. You are going to see a great move of God. And I even see you moving with some children and ministering unto them, and seeing the Gifts of the Spirit released even in the children. And they begin to move out and minister to each other and you are going to be very influential in that area. God is going to use you in that area."* This prophecy came in August 1992, while we were enjoying the move we had made earlier to Elijah Centre. Things were going very well for us as a family while we were in this new ministry.

The following year, an Afro-Canadian pastor ministered at our church and shared a testimony of incredible and staggering proportions. Little did we know that the Lord was at it again, and the course of events that would follow, would change our lives forever. Please indulge me as I share this preacher's story with you. Here in a nutshell, is my recollection of the details:

He was born to an African mother who left him in a heap to die, as she did not want the baby. During her pregnancy she made several attempts at abortion, but without success. Found by some priests, they took him into their monastery where he grew up. During his upbringing, he dreamt of being a minister of the gospel and when he became a man, went to seminary and graduated to a pastorate in his nation. While in that pastorate, the Lord spoke to him about a journey that he would make into Canada and gave him the date of his departure. Excited, he went about telling everyone about it, but the day came, and to his dismay and embarrassment, nothing happened.

Subsequently, the Lord gave him another vision and in that vision he went to Canada and the Lord showed him the home in which he would live; it was very detailed, down to the wall paper, drapes and bedspread. The Lord also told him the date he would leave his native homeland. However, this time the Lord commanded that he tell no one about his visitation.

This man left Africa on the exact day that the Lord had declared to him. On his arrival at Pearson's International Airport in Toronto, Canada he was detained by Immigration Officials as he did not have, nor did he know of its requirement, a Canadian Visa. However, while in the washroom the Lord spoke to him, declaring that He, the Lord, wanted him in Canada and that he should walk back to the Immigration Officer and tell him that his transportation had arrived. He went and did exactly as the Lord told him and to his surprise, they stamped his passport and released him. Not knowing anyone, and not knowing where to go, he momentarily sat down in the arrival lobby. All of a sudden this tall, white gentleman approached him, asking *"Is this your first time in Canada?"* to which he replied in the affirmative of course. Being in the height of winter and not wearing any protective clothing, this stranger asked if he had a winter jacket and upon learning that he had none, he proceeded to his car and brought back a jacket, which was the correct fit.

The Lord that we serve; Jesus Christ, is an awesome God! You see, earlier in the day, this *"unsaved"* Canadian went to work on a construction site, when a sudden feeling of not wanting to work, came upon him. He asked for and received the day off and he decided (or so he thought) to visit the airport and spend the day watching airplanes take off and land. Enroute to the airport, he passed by a departmental store downtown and saw this short coat on a manikin in the showcase. Being already upset, he said to himself "don't they know that there are tall people living in the earth?" Being tall himself, and out of pure frustration he purchased this coat and threw it in his car.

This "unsaved" Canadian then took this destiny bound, unknown African to his home and fed and accommodated him for the next two weeks. After this time the Lord spoke to the African minister that He wanted him in a place called Edmonton. He inquired of his host, who promptly purchased a ticket, gave him some money and sent him on his way. On his arrival in Edmonton he initially stayed at a Bread and Breakfast facility, and during that time decided to attend a Full Gospel Businessmen Meeting scheduled to take place that week. While at this meeting a woman approached him, and to his complete surprise declared *"you are the man, you are the man"*. He later learnt, that there was a group of Christians meeting at a home who were praying for the Lord to send them a leader, and two of the sisters from that fellowship had visions of the same man (him) coming to lead them. Now please understand; these are white people living in Edmonton, Canada, praying for a leader whom the Lord takes from all the way over in Africa, of different colour and ethnic upbringing, in answer to their prayer. He went with the women, and they gave him a room to live in and yes, you guessed it, *there it was, the very same bedspread, drapes and wallpaper that he was shown in the vision.* He went on to lead this church into the Will and Presence of the Lord. The church is still operating today, although under a different name. There is quite a bit more to his testimony but I will not go into it at this time. Maybe I will provide more details, if the Lord permits me to write an autobiography.

As this minister shared this incredible testimony, we listened and were blessed, but had absolutely no inkling of the sequence of events that were about to take place.

Later that year I was leaving my job to step into "full-time" ministry, and as was my custom, I went up to Fort George (a high place overlooking the city of Port of Spain, Trinidad), early one morning to pray. The events of that morning changed my life forever. Another brother was with me that morning, and as we prayed I began interceding for this Afro-Canadian minister, and although I was praying in the Spirit, I knew that I was praying for him. During that time of prayer the Lord spoke to me and said "This minister is about to loose his place in Canada and I will be sending you to replace him." As it turned out, later that year, this minister was once again visiting our island and as I transported him from the airport, I told him that the Lord had me to pray earnestly for him. His response jolted me when he said "I have given up my ministry in Canada and I now operate from the United States."

From that time onward there was an acceleration of the Lord's plan to move us into Canada. There were several confirmations and divine occurrences that culminated in our migrating to Canada in 1997, where we are seeing the Hand of the Lord directing us.

To date there have been several *"Divine Connections"* that have taken place since arriving in Canada; permit to share one with you.

It all began in August of 1998 as I was deeply engrossed in designing our ministry's website, when I got engaged in a random chat request on the ICQ program. Little did I know at that time, that the Holy Spirit was actually orchestrating what has now turned out to be a very significant entrance into the nation of Sri Lanka.

I vividly remember the person on the other end of the internet conversation, asking me (by typing) who I was and where was I from, to which I replied, I am a Pastor, ministering out of Vancouver, Canada. The response to my reply was *"Praise God, can you pray for me, as I am on the Internet looking for employment?"* I then inquired to whom I was communicating and the person responded that she was Christine from Sri Lanka.

As I was typing up a prayer, the Lord gave me a prophetic word for her, which I conveyed. I proceeded to tell her that the prophetic word would come to pass on or before August 31st, 1998!

About one week later, I was again contacted by Christine with very exciting news. She reported the following: "The very week you prayed and prophesied over my life we had a welcome home function for a relative who was returning from Germany. He was accompanied by a German friend who could not speak English, and found himself all alone at this function. Being able to speak a bit of German I decided to go over and communicate with him. Of course the gentleman was very elated and the next day I was asked if I would do some translating for him at some business meetings, to which I agreed.

Later that week this German man (who I then learnt was very wealthy and on a visit to negotiate some business deals) was about to depart and asked my relative how he could thank me for my work. My relative disclosed to him that I was not working and that I was a very good cook. This man offered to give me one million, yes one million dollars ($1,000,000.00) towards the establishment of a restaurant. When this news was related to me I was completely spellbound and immediately knew that this was the word that you had spoken to me over the Internet."

As it turned out, she did not take the million dollars but they agreed on an initial sum, so that she could make a start at the business. She began a small operation from her home and on August 31st, 1998 she got payment for her first contract. Again, Christine was absolutely amazed at the accuracy of the prophetic word.

From then on we would communicate often, and I prophesied to her that she would come into contact with a prayer group in her nation that will be a tremendous blessing to her. This too came to pass. In January of 1999, Christine contacted me via e-mail to ask if a woman by the name of Amrita had contacted me, to which I replied in the negative. She then informed me, that a born again, Spirit-Filled, Believer named Amrita had migrated from Sri Lanka to Vancouver, Canada whom she had asked to get in touch with me. I got Amrita's e-mail address from Christine and wrote to her. That afternoon Amrita got in touch with me. At this point in her lifeshe was suffering culture shock and was very unsettled in the wintry weather which was very alien to her, having lived in a tropical country. Having arrived as a Landed Immigrant, she had already decided to leave and return to Sri Lanka. I invited her out to church, and as it turned out she was not living too far from where we assembled. She arrived for the service and gave her testimony to the saints who were being kept abreast of this amazing sequence of events.

Around that same time I had a dream where I was in an unknown nation, when two men came up to me in a restaurant and begged me to come to their nation as I was needed there. They insisted that they will pay me very well and quoted a figure of a couple of million rupees or rubles. In the dream I did not know what nation's currency that was, but I knew that it was very low against the US dollar. As a matter of fact, the millions quoted only translated into a few thousand US dollars. I agreed to go to the nation and then awoke from the dream.

Awaking from this dream I was reminded of the account in the book of Acts about [42]Paul's visit into Macedonia and the establishing of the Philippian church. On speaking to Amrita later on, I learnt among other things that Christine and herself were first cousins and prior to her leaving for Vancouver, Canada she had no knowledge of our encounter on the Internet. In fact, she only learnt about it when she wrote Christine, informing her that she was looking to return to Sri Lanka. It was at that point that Christine related to her the events that took place, and encouraged her to contact me. I also learnt that the currency of Sri Lanka was the rupee. Amrita continued attending our ministry. As she was tremendously blessed, she gave her pastor in Sri Lanka our website and reported to him all that had taken place with her. Her Pastor later contacted me and we began relating, culminating in my making a ministry trip into that nation where the Lord showed Himself very strong. We continue relating to this ministry and are excited at the ways and doings of the Lord.

The "*Fortress Church*" is an awesome place and the Lord continues to raise up these types of churches in the earth. Following is an excerpt of what the Lord has done in the life of Amrita, who is truly a "*Divine Connection*" and a tremendous resource to what the Lord is doing through us.

Of mixed-faith parents I grew up a non-practicing Muslim - my father was Muslim by birth, atheist in belief and my mother a non-practicing Roman Catholic. Naturally then I received no spiritual guidance in my life and believed I was merely an addition to the world population, taught that all roads led to Rome, and good works got you into heaven. My occasional visits to the

---

[42] Acts 16:6-34

Roman Catholic Church on Christmas day inclined me more towards Christianity than Islam and as soon as I was given my freedom to choose, I became a Roman Catholic. I went through the motions of having water sprinkled on my face, was slapped by the Bishop and informed I had received the Holy Spirit. I showed up faithfully for mass every Sunday, novenas every Wednesday, but had no personal relationship with God and therefore did not experience His power in my life. I had no idea that God created me for His pleasure, for personal fellowship, with a purpose and also that I was of tremendous value to Him, valuable and precious enough that He counted and knew the number of hairs on my head.

"Unless the Lord builds the house, they labour in vain who build it" Psalm 127:1. Through the ages only one foundation has proved solid and dependable – Jesus Christ. And because it was not that way as I entered into marriage, I had a very turbulent one that produced a daughter and a son; it soon ended in a painful divorce that brought no justice.

A wounded and emotionally battered woman because of my many trials and difficult circumstances I faced at a very young age, I was furious at the world and God and foolishly thought I was "punishing" Him when I decided to stop even my occasional visits to church. I thought God could not deliver the goods to me in the day of trouble. And so taking my life into my own hands, I made all decisions and walked my own way. "*I*" was in charge!

I decided there was a better way than God's way and of course satan gleefully promoted the merits of hatred, bitterness and revenge towards all those who had hurt me in some way. Of course we all know the enemy sows seed in your heart in times of trouble. I think by now, because of my attitude and response many people thought I was beyond redemption. But then, they didn't know my *Redeemer and Restorer*!

In 1986 God mercifully got my attention through my 18-

month-old son – a mother's most vulnerable spot. A week into my new job I received a telephone call from home to say my son had an accident. I was told that a wooden cabinet packed with clothes had fallen on him. *"Return home immediately"* was the command. I trembled and shook at the possibility of my son dying or being seriously injured and was at the end of all hope –the ideal situation for divine intervention. I remember praying on the way home, and drawing upon the very limited understanding I had of Him said *"Lord, if you will save my baby, my life is yours"*. I didn't understand the meaning of this prayer nor did I realize the depth of the commitment, and the fact the Lord was going to hold me to that, just as He honours and performs every word and every promise He has given to us. My son was hospitalised a day for observation, and came out unscathed. I have journaled this as my very first experience of the power of God and His ability to hear and answer prayer.

Very soon after this incident, the Lord orchestrated it so that I attended a miracle service in a Pentecostal church – my very first Pentecostal experience! I liked what I heard – loved it in fact, and kept going back for more. I responded to an altar call and received Jesus into my heart. From that moment I had joy – a joy that caused me to sing aloud as I walked down the street – dance even, if not for the risk of being looked upon as a crazy Jane. Did the troubles go away? No. Did I expect it to? Yes, as a brand new Christian I did. I was to later learn that being a daughter of God did not give me immunity from suffering and troubles – but gave me sufficient grace to overcome every obstacle. As I continued as a new Christian, I struggled, without a revelatory knowledge of who God was and His overcoming power. I was unaware of the sanctification process and had no understanding of 2 Corinthians 3:18:

"But we all, with unveiled face, beholding as in a mirror the glory of the Lord, are being transformed into the same image from glory to glory, just as by the Spirit of the Lord."

It had nothing to do with the church or the preachers, but for whatever reason, I was unresponsive. I struggled with my old nature, because I was not looking into the mirror of God's word, and not having an intimate relationship with Him. I say this with hindsight. But at the time I felt pressurized, partly because I couldn't understand why I didn't change in an instant and partly because I was being closely watched by my whole family – for one wrong step, and the "*aha, aha*" plus the onus on me to walk the talk, without having the power to do so. I now know I had it from the minute I accepted Jesus, but just did not know how to call it forth into my life and its issues. Many times I didn't walk the talk, and had to contend with the snickering, innuendos and judgmental criticism. I suffered condemnation and felt hopeless at times, but through it all, I didn't realize it, but my faith was being built up. God was so wonderfully faithful – whenever I cried out to Him in critical and time sensitive situations, exercising reckless and radical faith, *He always showed up* and performed some incredible miracles – that would silence the mouths of my enemies.

In December 1998 I arrived in Vancouver as a landed immigrant. Little did I know I was entering a life-altering phase of my life. I was entering "my" season, "my" time ("kairos" in Greek) to become bold, receive overcoming power, and for my spiritual roots to go deep and also gather food and store. My first and immediate task was to find employment and then a church (*note the priority*). I was fast learning by the five responses to my one hundred and fifty resumes, that December was a laid back month in North America.

As for locating a church I absolutely refused to go the way of referring the yellow pages, and knew "*the right one would turn up*". By the third week of December (after having briefly contemplated calling the psychic hotline re prospects of a job) my cousin in Sri Lanka who had by then got to know of my depressed state because of no job and no church, emailed me the contact of a Michael Scantlebury who had set up a church in Vancouver and referred to him more as a prophet than a pastor.

Not having met a prophet or exposed to the prophetic ministry, I had no clue as to what she was talking about, but was happy about the prospect of making contact with a "*recommended*" man of God, which I did. He prayed with me over the phone and I knew immediately he was not a spiritless preacher, but a straight-forward man of God who sounded very serious about his calling and ministry. I liked that. To my utter delight I discovered that the church was not located in the backwoods of Vancouver, but within distance of where I lived. Vancouver being such a vast city, what were the odds of it being so? The church could have been anywhere. Already it had the scent of a "*Divine Connection*". Curious about this link, I questioned my cousin about how she knew this man of God and after I heard her story, I knew without a doubt, that the divine hand of God was pointing me in this direction. Please permit me to share it with you.

My cousin Christine was on the ICQ one night, when she connected with someone on line and inquired who it was. "I am a pastor ministering out of Vancouver" came the reply. Christine was thrilled to have contacted a pastor and asked him if he could pray for her as she was going through a very difficult period in her life at the time – she had no job and was quite depressed and frustrated. This pastor prayed for her and not only that, gave her a prophetic word that by a certain date, she would be given an opportunity for business in a particular field. They continued to chat on line. On the prophesied date, Christine was offered a financed business partnership involving a sizeable sum of money. She was astonished and amazed at the accuracy of the prophetic word.

All this began in June 1998. No one knew about this, least of all I because Christine and I were not on speaking terms until the day I left Sri Lanka, when a higher power urged me to put things right with our relationship. Had I not responded to the prompting of the Holy Spirit, I would have surely missed out on all that God had planned for me.

I attended my first service and have journaled it as my first exposure to spiritual warfare. I tried to enjoy this totally alien music, the stomping of feet and made a feeble attempt to enter into the "freedom of the spirit and moving in the spirit". Though it was something new to me, I was tremendously blessed; there was power in the words being released – in the proclamation and declarations through song and I was already feeling empowered and strengthened in my spirit ready to conquer! When it came to impartation of the Word, I sat spell bound at the revelation this preacher was imparting – I was scrambling to grab all that I could – this was good bread, fresh bread and I was suddenly hungry. On my very first day I felt "fully satisfied and *"filled"* in my spirit, had a sense of family and realized how divinely the Lord had led me to this house. How mindful of the Lord to provide just what I needed for the condition of my soul at the time. "And I will give you shepherds according to my heart, who will feed you with knowledge and understanding" Jeremiah 3:15. Whilst this verse of scripture has deeper meaning, and my pastor could probably preach a whole sermon on this one verse, this is what the Lord literally did for me by bringing me under such a ministry.

"Katakismos" is Greek for edify, equip, help shape the church or individual and I was being *"katakismos-ed"* – there was an immediate and spontaneous conviction in my spirit. At the end of the service I was prayed over, especially for a job opening.

The Lord was at work almost immediately. In the beginning of February, I was offered employment at the University of British Columbia. It was as if this position was created for me, and had my name stamped on it. Here's why - I was cautioned that my boss was a difficult person to work for and the position was like a revolving door - no one wanted it. One secretary had lasted just two hours. But by now I was feeling quite confident because the power of God was operative in my life in a new way, and I had no fear. I knew deep inside that no demon could stand in the way of what God was giving me.

On my first day at work I was introduced as the Secretary who would be working for the beast, and received condolences instead of congratulations. Well, I thought, I had the weapon for the *"beast"*. Such was his reputation. And so as my spirit feasted week after week, the eyes of my understanding began to open and I grasped an awareness of the power of God, which was wholly available to every child of His. Pastor Michael kept pounding into us the truth of who we were in Christ and I had no choice but to believe it, trust it and practice it. I became conversant with spiritual warfare and with my pastor leading the way, learnt how not to back down and how not to give demons control over my life. I became conscious of the fact that for a good part of my Christian life I was living in poverty while there was credit stacked up against my name in heaven, and accepting defeat when God had made a way for victory. Suddenly words like destiny and purpose took on a whole new meaning – there was such a stirring in my spirit. I was coming alive.

The manner in which the Holy Spirit was imparting the word of God through this man, caused an insatiable hunger and thirst in my spirit – a condition that drove me to discipline my spiritual life and commit to studying His word and being in His presence. Eager to be used of Him and in search of destiny, I sought Him day after day. However since the vessel He uses, He has to first clean, God began to entreat me to surrender all to Him, assuring me that my heart and life though wounded by man was safe in His hands. I began to trust Him. Up to this time bible study and being in His presence was not a priority and for the very first time in my life I faithfully gave the Lord the first hours of my day, and as I did so, 2 Corinthians 3:18 began its process.

"But we all, with unveiled face, beholding as in a mirror the glory of the Lord, are being transformed into the same image from glory to glory, just as by the Spirit of the Lord." (Italics added)

The Holy Spirit journeyed with me down the road of my past. We stopped at every door I had firmly shut and built defences around. He brought my attention to the rocks I had gathered over the years and together through a process, made them into pebbles and even presently He is dredging and siphoning them out. I couldn't refuse Him access, because by now He had me totally surrendered and I was in an *"all of you and none of me"* relationship with Him. I discovered we don't receive more of the Spirit – we give Him more of us. And He wants ALL of us.

There were occasions He would show me wrong things I did twenty years ago and right there at a bus stop, I would respond in tearful repentance. To a strong willed, independent and stubborn individual such as me, surrendering was a whole new and difficult experience.

In July 1999 I went back to Sri Lanka – not hoping to return. It was my intention to submit my resignation before I left, but a dear Christian friend of mine at UBC (University of British Columbia) suggested I throw a *"fleece"* and request for a leave of absence instead. Just like my pastor she felt in her spirit that I was meant to stay, but my "still being transformed" independent and strong willed mind was made up – I wanted to leave, for various reasons. Actually my pastor very definitely told me as he prayed that I was coming back. I asked for and received a leave of absence for 6 weeks. After 5 weeks I emailed my boss to say I had to regretfully submit my resignation and was making arrangements to permanently remain in Sri Lanka. Imagine then my utter surprise to receive a reply from my boss worded this way – *"I have discussed the matter of your resignation with the Administrative Manager and since we consider you a valuable member of the team, would like you to return to your position. We are willing to extend your leave of absence up to January of 2000."*

Friends, the Hand of the Lord is still able to perform wonders – He is the same yesterday, today and forever. Here was I, an employee of just four months (of which three months was probationary), in one of the best university's in Canada, working for a supposedly difficult boss, and *asked* to come back? Can anyone other than God perform something so phenomenal? Right in the midst of employees being laid off and a high unemployment rate, He blesses His own – in the midst of the famine. Remember we are called to dwell in high places, to be the head and not the tail and our resources are not of this world. Isn't that wonderful?

As soon as I read the email my mind was made up – Unmistakably God was saying, "I want you back there". I responded, "Okay Lord, I will not fight you, because you always win and I lose, and that's the way I want it to be. Have your way, now and always." He had tamed my heart! I returned to Canada in November 1999, and how glorious life has been for me – even better than the former. I am not referring to purely material blessing, but my experience of His power, provision and deliverance. My boss and I have a wonderful working relationship, which in fact causes many raised eyebrows and surprised looks from my co-workers. I was once asked the secret of my success with him and I replied it was because of prayer and the power of God to work all things for my good. What the Lord blesses is good, is very, very good.

Whilst God frees us from the penalty of sin at conversion He also begins to destroy the power of sin in our daily life. The *Great Restorer* is now at work in me – casting down the high things and building up the low. As He continues to invite me to wash away my anger and pride, fear and envy, guilt and shame in the pure stream of His forgiveness, I am being healed, restored and transformed, hallelujah. God's Spirit and power is now operative in my life; instead of whimpering, "Woe is me" I have learnt to speak the word and will of God into my situations and have seen Him deliver over and over again. *"Lord I will obey you"* has become a way of life for me. From the moment the eyes of my understanding were enlightened my life began to change. As I study His word and sit in His presence daily, He renews my thoughts and heart. How true is the scripture in Hosea 4:6 "My people are destroyed for lack of knowledge". I know I almost was.

Not just purifying, He is also building the ruins of my life, I find that I am able to love and pray for those I formerly despised and disliked. He IS restoring me and I am fully confident, by the power of the Holy Spirit that I will fulfill my destiny and accomplish the will of God. God Himself is fire and is cleaning and torching all that needs to burn and He won't quit until it's all cleansed. The process has only begun – we have a long road ahead of us. Elder Scantlebury always emphasizes to us that we need struggles in order for destiny to come forth, and his life is a fitting example of that. Trials, testings and tribulations will come to all. God will send some and the devil will send some, but all of those will be used by the Almighty towards His end and purpose. God is greater than any trial you may be facing right now; relinquish control of your life and do nothing that diminishes His greatness. Do not allow trials to obscure your faith, but begin to see life in terms of what God can do through you – a very limited and flawed human being.

A Christian it is said is like a tea bag – he is not much good until he has been through some hot water! No matter what tomorrow may bring, you are part of an unshakeable Kingdom. Be grateful for receiving a Kingdom that cannot be shaken. In this season He is allowing kingdoms to be shaken so that men and women might discover the one Kingdom that is unshakeable. If you have moved away from the Lord and ceased to be dependent on Him, enter through the door of repentance, into His presence – the only place where you belong, where you will find strength and hope and peace. If it is something painful, be sure that He has permitted it because He can use it. Have the moral courage to stand alone if necessary and be willing to be in the minority for God – first and foremost, you belong to Him.

The God who made the vast universe is interested in the details of your life and has plans for your highest good. Believe that. *Be a thermostat and not a thermometer – a thermometer merely registers the temperature, a thermostat changes it*! Begin a journey of discovering the Holy Spirit's power and tap into the resources stored up for you in the heart of God. Discover not only His name, but also His Nature. Many of us are dying spiritually because we are looking the wrong way; we look at the ruin instead of heaven's resources; we see the gloom instead of the glory. El Shaddai (*God The Enough*) is always ready to breathe into situations and circumstances where a miracle is required. When He does then the word *impossible* becomes *Him-possible*.

Davidic Example Of A Fortress Church

David's rise to King and what he does when it happens presents to us a wonderful picture of the "*Fortress Church*".

"Then all the tribes of Israel came to David at Hebron and spoke, saying, "Indeed we are your bone and your flesh. Also, in time past, when Saul was king over us, you were the one who led Israel out and brought them in; and the LORD said to you, 'You shall shepherd My people Israel, and be ruler over Israel.' "Therefore all the elders of Israel came to the king at Hebron, and King David made a covenant with them at Hebron before the LORD. And they anointed David king over Israel. David was thirty years old when he began to reign, and he reigned forty years. In Hebron he reigned over Judah seven years and six months, and in Jerusalem he reigned thirty-three years over all Israel and Judah. And the king and his men went to Jerusalem against the Jebusites, the inhabitants of the land, who spoke to David, saying, "You shall not come in here; but the blind and the lame will repel you," thinking, "David cannot come in here." Nevertheless David took the stronghold of Zion (that is, the City of David). Now David said on that day, "Whoever climbs up by way of the water shaft and defeats the Jebusites (the lame and the blind, who are hated by David's soul), he shall be chief and captain." Therefore they say, "The blind and the lame shall not come into the house." Then David dwelt in the stronghold, and called it the City of David. And David built all around from the Millo and inward. So David went on and became great, and the LORD God of hosts was with him." 2 Samuel 5:1-10

At this point, David was King over Judah where he had reigned seven and a half years. Saul had died, and the prophetic word that Samuel had given to him some twenty-three years before, is about to be fulfilled. However, he dwelt in Hebron for seven and a half years before the word came to pass. Hebron is a very powerful place in the plan of God for our lives.

HEBRON

Although Hebron is a physical city, it carries a powerful spiritual dimension in God. It can represent the following: Hebron in the Hebrew is translated - confederacy, from which the noun confederate, is derived, and carries the following meaning - To unite in a confederacy or to be united in a league. So from this we can derive that *Hebron* represented a place of unity.

Remember the children of Israel's journey from Egypt to the Promised Land? The first encounter they had with it was about forty days after they left Egypt and Moses sent out the twelve spies. This is what happened:

1. Numbers 13: They entered through the south where Hebron was and they came upon the sons of Anak; *giants*, and ten came back with an evil report that they could not take the land. They saw themselves as *grasshoppers*! Only Joshua and Caleb ("Praise & Worship" and "Doubly Fruitful" for that's what their names meant) came back with a good report.

2. They went to the place of *unity* and came back divided, and for forty years wandered through the wilderness before the Lord killed the *"unbelievers"*, the ones that fostered disunity. Only Joshua and Caleb remained, and a *new generation* was raised up to go in with them.

3. After forty years they are about to enter the Promised Land; however, this time they do not enter from the south but from the north – entirely in the opposite direction – and the first place that they encountered was Jericho, and the last place they came to was Hebron.

4. Hebron then can represent one of the final frontiers for the Church.

Here Are Some Of The Other Dimensions Of Hebron:

1. It is a place of separation from earthbound Christianity into one's true destiny and purpose – Abraham visited that place and entered into his true purpose after he separated from Lot his cousin – Genesis 13

2. It is the place of a name change – Abram was changed to Abraham, and Sari was changed to Sarah

3. It is a place of declared destiny, a Place of *transition* into a higher realm: - Even though Abraham dwelt, he was still looking for a city whose maker and builder was God– In essence he was looking for the Church.

David is in a place of transition, as Samuel had prophesied over him some twenty-three years before, that the Lord had chosen him to lead his people Israel. He got his first anointing in his earthly father's house; he received his second anointing in Hebron and now he is receiving his third anointing that will take him into his ultimate purpose – to lead all of God's people.

It was here that David made a *Covenant* with Leadership –

Verse 3 - This third anointing pushes us to the ultimate – it is similar to the anointing by *fire* – it is the place of serious commitment.

It was from Hebron, and after his third anointing, that David rises up to take the *stronghold of Zion* – now he could not live his life in transition – this was the real deal; this is what he was born for. However, as we would see, there is always confrontation to the purpose of God.

The Blind And The Lame - Verses 6-10
The word for lame in the Hebrew is translated HESISTANT – people that refuse to function in a forceful way – *"From the days of John the Baptist until now, the kingdom of heaven has been forcefully advancing, and forceful men lay hold of it."* Matthew 11:12 NIV (Italics added) – *passivity does not advance the Kingdom of God*! It only locks us into Religious Activity. David destroys the Lame and the Blind – the Word declares that they were hated of David's soul. He then goes on and establishes *Zion (a type of the Church)*, as a place of *dominion* for God's people! This was very prophetic as he was proclaiming what the Church should be like in the earth.

A.W. Tozer says: *"The church has surrendered her once lofty concept of God and has substituted for it one so low, so ignoble, as to be utterly unworthy of thinking, worshipping men. Not deliberately, but little by little, without her knowledge; and her very unawareness only makes her situation all the more tragic."*

Dynamics Of The Fortress Church
"This is what Isaiah son of Amoz saw concerning Judah and Jerusalem: *In the last days the mountain of the LORD's temple will be established as chief among the mountains*; it will be raised above the hills, *and all nations will stream to it. Many peoples will come and say, "Come, let us go up to the mountain of the LORD*, to the house of the God of Jacob. He will teach us his ways, so that we

may walk in his paths." *The law will go out from Zion, the word of the LORD from Jerusalem.* He will judge between the nations and will settle disputes for many peoples. *They will beat their swords into plowshares and their spears into pruning hooks.* Nation will not take up sword against nation, nor will they train for war anymore. Isaiah 2:1-4 NIV (Italics added)

"Great is the LORD, and most worthy of praise, in the city of our God, his holy mountain. It is beautiful in its loftiness, the joy of the whole earth. Like the utmost heights of Zaphon is Mount Zion, the city of the Great King. God is in her citadels; *he has shown himself to be her fortress.* When *the kings joined forces, when they advanced together, they saw* [her] *and were astounded; they fled in terror. Trembling seized them there, pain like that of a woman in labour.* You destroyed them like ships of Tarshish shattered by an east wind. *As we have heard, so have we seen* in the city of the LORD Almighty, in the city of our God: God makes her secure forever. Selah Within your temple, O God, we meditate on your unfailing love. Like your name, O God, your praise reaches to the ends of the earth; your right hand is filled with righteousness. *Mount Zion rejoices, the villages of Judah are glad because of your judgments.* Walk about Zion, go around her, count her towers, consider well her ramparts, view her citadels, *that you may tell of them to the next generation.* For this God is our God for ever and ever; he will be our guide even to the end. Psalm 48 NIV (Parenthesis and Italics added)

God is Great in the Fortress Church and worthy of all praise. It is beautiful in its *loftiness* or *elevation*.

Loftiness – this word is not to be used in the sense of being proud or haughty but it is to be used in the sense of position; a place of elevation.

Mt Zion – The Church is beautiful because of its *elevation,* *its loftiness, its position*! As a matter of fact, the terminology "Mt Zion on the sides of the North" in Hebrew depicts *Elevation or Height*.

Elevation or Height is very important in the spirit realm. As seen in Isaiah 2:1-4, the world is going *up* to Zion, (The "Fortress Church")! This *up lifestyle* is not that which is consistent with the world; it must be different; it must cause the world to turn their heads and take notice at you. This is awesome, as all of this is happening in the last days – certainly we qualify to be this type of church.

It is imperative that we understand that *the spirit realm runs by rank or position*. The Apostle Paul in writing to the church at Ephesus made this very clear:

"Therefore I also, after I heard of your faith in the Lord Jesus and your love for all the saints, do not cease to give thanks for you, making mention of you in my prayers: that the God of our Lord Jesus Christ, the Father of glory, may give to you the spirit of wisdom and revelation in the knowledge of Him, the eyes of your understanding being enlightened; that you may know what is the hope of His calling, what are the riches of the glory of His inheritance in the saints, and what is the exceeding greatness of His power toward us who believe, according to the working of His mighty power which He worked in Christ when He raised Him from the dead and seated Him at His right hand in the heavenly places, *far above all* principality and power and might and dominion, and every name that is named, not only in this age but also in that which is to come. And He put all things under His feet, *and gave Him to be head over all things to the church*, which is His body, the fullness of Him who fills all in all. And you He made alive, who were dead in trespasses and sins, in which you once walked according to the course of this world, according to the prince of the power of the air, the spirit who now works in the sons of disobedience, among whom also we all once conducted ourselves in the lusts of our flesh, fulfilling the desires of the flesh and of the mind, and were by nature children of wrath, just as the others. But God, who is rich in mercy, because of His great love with which He loved us, even when we were dead in trespasses, *made us alive together with Christ* (by grace you have been saved), *and raised us up together, and made us sit together in the heavenly places in Christ Jesus.*" Ephesians 1:15 - 2:6 (Italics added)

In describing the Lord's position, the Apostle Paul uses very strong and expressive language - *far above all!* Jesus is not just above all principalities, powers, might and dominion He is *at an extreme distance above* them. Apostles are mandated to bring the church into a clear understanding of this fact. They want to see every Believer conformed to the Image of Christ. The Apostle Paul's earnest cry for the saints was that they saw, comprehended and entered into the awesome revelation of "Christ in you the hope of glory." Paul accentuated that fact when he went on to establish that when Jesus was positioned *far above all*, we were *raised up together with Him!* We are positioned in the same place that Jesus is and we must know and realize this.

As the Blacksmiths sharpen the Lord's battleaxes, we have to fight from our position of *authority – above all powers!*

Let me reemphasize the fact that the spirit realm works by an *internal sense of your position – position is vital.* We just have to know this and be very conscious of the fact, because the devil will try everything possible to negate this fact.

Jesus is *lifted up over every other* name. *He has the highest rank or position.* When we pray in the name of Jesus it is *from a position* we are praying, and not just a religious phrase we are using – not just something we add on to our prayers for power.

In Jesus Name! – It Is A Spiritual Location From Which We Function – It Is A Lifestyle – It Is An Identity

We cannot function in the spirit realm with condemnation – *we must be confident in our position in Him* – we must know our significance in *Him*! This is the mentality of apostolic people in the "*Fortress Church*".

The Reality Of What Jesus Accomplished

"Therefore He says: "When He ascended on high, He led captivity captive, And gave gifts to men." (Now this, "He ascended"—what does it mean but that He also first descended into the lower parts of the earth? He who descended is also the One who ascended far above all the heavens, that He might fill all things.) Ephesians 4:8-10

• He descended then He *arose*

• He went into the deepest depths of hell and then arose

• Every place the soles of your feet tread it is yours

• *Jesus* has control and authority over every realm from heaven to the lowest part of hell

We as Born-Again Believers have the same authority because of Jesus – We *sit with Him* in Heavenly places.

For those of you reading this book and still have problems with condemnation, hear me – this is the hour for you to *break away* from your past life of condemnation! Remember *He ascended that He might fill all things!* And He has taken us with Him, as we are also seated in heavenly places *in* Christ.

The next facet we see of this end-time Church is the intensity of its warfare; as the kings of the earth join forces to seek its destruction:

> "When the kings joined forces, when they advanced together, they saw [her] and were astounded; they fled in terror. Trembling seized them there, pain like that of a woman in labour. You destroyed them like ships of Tarshish shattered by an east wind." NIV Psalm 48:4-7

These kings of the earth are demonic. They assemble and advance against the *"Fortress Church"*. These are not little insignificant devils that cause pastors to divorce their wives and marry their secretaries. No! These are big devils; they are high ranking demonic powers and they will seek to dismantle, disjoint, and completely destroy the *"Fortress Church"*. This is why every local church needs to have the apostolic dimension in it. Part of the apostolic career is the ability to dismantle demonic thrones and powers. The apostolic anointing can dismantle, penetrate and dismantle inaccurate mindsets and thought patterns established by these "demonic kings of the earth". The Apostle Paul effectively describes this apostolic dimension when he said:

> "For the weapons of our warfare are not carnal but mighty in God for pulling down strongholds, casting down arguments and every high thing that exalts itself against the knowledge of God, bringing every thought into captivity to the obedience of Christ, and being ready to punish all disobedience when your obedience is fulfilled. 2 Corinthians 10:4-6

This new apostolic Church (*Fortress Church*) that is rising in the earth, is awesome. The demonic kings of the earth *saw it* (the implication here is that they saw and understood what was happening. They saw and heard). They scrutinized it; they carefully checked out this *"Fortress Church"*; this *stronghold* – this was not a casual looking, this was intense. Look at Ephesians 3:8-12

> "...this grace was given, that I should preach among the Gentiles the unsearchable riches of Christ, and to make all see what is the fellowship of the mystery, which from the

beginning of the ages has been hidden in God who created all things through Jesus Christ; *to the intent that now
the manifold wisdom of God might be made known by the
church to the principalities and powers in the heavenly
places*, according to the eternal purpose which He accomplished in Christ Jesus our Lord, in whom we have bold-
ness and access with confidence through faith in Him."
(Italics added)

Some may argue that the reference to *principalities and powers* is not demonic but righteous angels. This cannot be, as every
other [43]mention of that term denotes demonic activity.

When these demonic kings saw and heard they *marvelled*! It
is the word *astonished*. They were in *confusion and consternation*.

The kingdom of darkness is tormented by a *"Fortress
Church"* - the result, *they fled in terror* (NIV); this is what a
"Fortress Church" does to the enemy. The Church of the Lord
Jesus Christ is rising in the earth, to its place of pre-ordained
strength and beauty. There are more dimensions to this church
that is emerging.

"As we have heard, So we have seen In the city of the LORD of
hosts, In the city of our God: God will establish it forever.
Selah" Psalm 48:8 (Italics added)

As We Have Heard So Have We Seen
There has been too much hearing and no seeing, and the
Lord God Almighty is changing all of that. This new "apostolic
reformation" as some would prefer to call it, is changing the face
of the Church. In this Fortress Church the face of man is disap-
pearing and instead is becoming the place where you can SEE
the Lord. This type of Church is not built around programs or
man or personalities; it is built on vision that is centered in the

---

[43] Romans 8:38, Ephesians 6:12, Colossians 1:16 & Colossians 2:15

Lord. *It Is A Place Where The Walk Matches The Talk!* It is an Apostolic Church that can decode and bring to reality the mysteries of the Lord. Similar to the Apostle Peter on the Day of Pentecost in Acts 2:14-16:

> "But Peter, standing up with the eleven, lifted up his voice, and said unto them, Ye men of Judaea, and all ye that dwell at Jerusalem, be this known unto you, and hearken to my words: For these are not drunken, as ye suppose, seeing it is but the third hour of the day. *But this is that* which was spoken by the prophet Joel." KJV (Italics added)

What you have heard, we now bring into manifestation, Apostle Peter was declaring, and we need to do the same. The *"Fortress Church"* allows the Word to *become* flesh and live through the Saints. This is why we must allow the *Blacksmiths* to return and do what the Lord has assigned to them so that this Church, this *"Fortress Church"* can fully rise in the earth.

This *Fortress Church* progresses into a place of what can be best described as *Mature Joy*, a joy that reaches beyond the initial [44]Joy of Salvation.

Mature Joy

> "Within your temple, O God, we meditate on your *unfailing love*. Like your name, O God, your praise reaches to the ends of the earth; your right hand is filled with righteousness. *Mount Zion rejoices*, the villages of *Judah are glad because of your judgments*. Psalm 48:9-11 (Italics added)

This type of joy is produced as a result of God's judgement. Judgement here is not speaking about God's punishment. It is referring to the Lord's *justice or decision*. This is the joy that

---

[44] Isaiah 12:3

results from an *obedient lifestyle* – that comes from *righteous living*. This is what happens as the Apostles come alongside the other "Five-Fold" ministry gifts, assisting in the perfecting of the Saints; bringing us into the fullness of the measure of the stature of Jesus Christ. It is maturity when we can submit to the Hand and Process of Almighty God – it is immaturity when we cannot submit and be brought under the Mighty Hand of God, and under the scrutiny of God.

Remember it is Righteousness, Peace and Joy in the Holy Ghost! We must all be in the grip of a mighty process, a process of change through the Hands of a Mighty God! There is Joy because of God's Judgement! This Mature Joy is produced when we walk accurate in God. When we allow our steps to be ordered and ordained by Him.

This Maturity Produces Generational Blessings!
The *"Fortress Church"* is an exemplar, model or prototype Church. We must declare that it is possible to build a Strong Church. A Church that reclaims its *Generational Power*, a Church that can last through the generations, with a sense of purpose and direction.

The *"Fortress Church"* seeks to destroy the spirit that causes the next generation to be lost. That happened under Joshua and so many others, through the history of the church.

"Now Joshua the son of Nun, the servant of the LORD, died when he was one hundred and ten years old. And they buried him within the border of his inheritance at Timnath Heres, in the mountains of Ephraim, on the north side of Mount Gaash. When all that generation had been gathered to their fathers, *another generation arose after them who did not know the LORD nor the work which He had done for Israel.* Then the children of Israel did evil in the sight of the LORD, and served the Baals; and they forsook the LORD God of their fathers, who had brought them out of the land of Egypt; and they followed other gods from among the gods of the people who were all around them, and they bowed down to them; and they provoked the LORD to anger." Judges 2:8-12 (Italics added)

From that time the Lord allowed judges to lead the people, when His true desire was to have kings (45a type of the apostolic), over them. And when the judge followed the Lord, they did what was right and when he did not, they did not. There was no internal self-government formed in the people.

The *"Fortress Church"* will be a true *"Fathering"* Church with an Elijah spirit, where the hearts of the fathers have truly been turned to the children and the heart of the children turned to their fathers; resulting in true *"Generational Blessings"*.

Another dimension of this *"Fortress Church"* is the grace anointing from the Lord, to bring in the Harvest. This end time Church is also spoken of in the book of Isaiah:

"The word that Isaiah the son of Amoz saw concerning Judah and Jerusalem. *Now it shall come to pass in the latter days That the mountain of the LORD's house Shall be established on the top of the mountains, And shall be exalted above the hills; And all nations shall flow to it.* Many people shall come and say, "*Come, and let us go up to the mountain of the LORD,* To the house of the God of Jacob; He will teach us His ways, And we shall walk in His paths." *For out of Zion shall go forth the law,* And the word of the LORD from Jerusalem. He shall judge between the nations, And rebuke many people; *They shall beat their swords into plowshares, And their spears into pruning hooks;* Nation shall not lift up sword against nation, Neither shall they learn war anymore." Isaiah

---

[45] For more on this you can read the author's book "Five Pillars of the Apostolic – Ordering details at the end of this book.

2:1-4 (Italics added)

This is so awesome! The Prophet Isaiah is given this panoramic view of the Last Day Church and it is just powerful. We would all agree that Isaiah is indeed speaking about the Church, the Lord's House, Zion if you will, of that there should be no doubt.

Like was earlier said, the Last Day Church will be in an elevated position, her status of being *"seated in heavenly places in Christ Jesus"* will be accentuated in these times.

Contrary to some popular opinions, the Last Day Church will see the nations coming to her for guidance. This is already occurring in some quarters as leaders of nations seek out the counsel of godly men. This Church is described as established and exalted. This is the mandate upon the *"Five-Fold"* ministry, to bring the Church of the Living God to a place of ordained strength and maturity. I love how the Apostle Paul declares it in the following passage:

> *"Now to Him who is able to establish you according to my gospel and the preaching of Jesus Christ, according to the revelation of the mystery kept secret since the world began but now has been made manifest, and by the prophetic Scriptures has been made known to all nations, according to the commandment of the everlasting God,* for obedience to the faith - to God, alone wise, be glory through Jesus Christ forever. Amen." Romans 16:25-27 (Italics added)

The Prophet goes on to declare that the law will proceed out of Zion. The law here is not referring to legalism but instead it is referring to lifestyle principles. This *"Fortress Church"* will be a place where the Saints will be walking in *"Lifestyle Christianity"*, not Sunday morning theatrics. They will demonstrate the quality of life for which our Lord Jesus Christ purchased with His Blood.

However, there is something of tremendous note that occurs in this end time, *"Fortress Church"*; a command goes forth for them to *beat their swords into plowshares, And their spears into pruning hooks.* This is powerful for two reasons as it implies the following:

Firstly, in order for the Church to get to the place of being established on top of the mountain, she had to war her way to it. She arrived at the top of the mountain with sword and spear in hand. This is why the church today must have Blacksmiths within her if we are to arrive at this pre-determined destination of ruling among the nations. Apostles are being released by the Lord in this hour, to sharpen us in understanding the Will and Purpose of the Lord. Knowledge is power, which is why Daniel declared:

"Those who do wickedly against the covenant he shall corrupt with flattery; *but the people who know their God shall be strong, and carry out great exploits.* And those of *the people who understand shall instruct many..."* Daniel 11:32-33 (Italics added)

Remember, we the Saints, are the Lord's Battleaxes. We are the ones He uses in accomplishing His will. As we are sharpened in our understanding of Him and His perfect will, we can then execute His written judgements. There is a massive warfare for the minds of men. The mind is the biggest and greatest battleground, for the Word of God declares "For *as he thinks* in his heart, *so is he.*" Proverbs 23:6 (Italics added). The Apostle Paul also describes it this way:

"For *the weapons of our warfare* are not carnal but mighty in God for pulling down strongholds, *casting down arguments and every high thing that exalts itself against the knowledge of God, bringing every thought into captivity to the obedience of Christ*, and being ready to punish all disobedience when your obedience is fulfilled." 2 Corinthians 10:4-6 (Italics added)

He clearly shows us that the battle is in the thought realm. Hence, part of the mandate given to the end-time Apostles is to destroy wrong mindsets, concepts and principles that have been established in the minds of the saints, and replace them with correct ones.

Secondly, when this is accomplished, we are going to see one of the largest harvests of souls the world has ever seen. The command goes forth for the saints to *beat their swords into plowshares, And their spears into pruning hooks.* Their weapons of warfare are now returned to farming implements; which will be used in the greatest harvest of the ages.

CHAPTER 6

THE POWER OF UNITY

"**B**ehold, *how good and how pleasant it is For brethren to dwell together in unity*! It is like *the precious oil* upon the head, Running down on the beard, The beard of Aaron, Running down on the edge of his garments. It is like *the dew of Hermon*, Descending upon *the mountains of Zion*; For there the LORD commanded the blessing—Life forevermore." Psalm 133 (Italics added)

As the Church of Jesus Christ gives operational room to the Lord's end-time Apostles, we will finally see the fulfillment of that powerful promise in the book of Ephesians:

"I, therefore, the prisoner of the Lord, beseech you to walk worthy of the calling with which you were called, with all lowliness and gentleness, with longsuffering, bearing with one another in love, endeavoring to keep the unity of the Spirit in the bond of peace. There is one body and one Spirit, just as you were called in one hope of your calling; one Lord, one faith, one baptism; one God and Father of all, who is above all, and through all, and in you all. But to each one of us grace was given according to the measure of Christ's gift. 8 Therefore He says: "When He ascended on high, He led captivity captive, And gave gifts to men." (Now this, "He ascended"—what does it mean but that He also first descended into the lower parts of the earth? He who descended is also the One who ascended far above all the heavens, that He might fill all things.) *And He Himself gave some to be apostles*, some prophets, some evangelists, and some pastors and teachers, *for the equipping of the saints for the work of ministry, for the edifying of the body of Christ, till we all come to the unity of the faith* and of the knowledge of the Son of God, to a perfect man, to the measure of the stature of the fullness of Christ; that we should no longer be children, tossed to and fro and carried about with every wind of doctrine, by the trickery of men, in the cunning craftiness of deceitful plotting, but, speaking the truth in love, may grow up in all things into Him who is the head—Christ— from whom the whole body, joined and knit together by what every joint supplies, according to the effective working by which every part does its share, causes growth of the body for the edifying of itself in love." Ephesians 4:1-16 (Italics added)

As we look across the vast expanse of what we call the Church, one cannot but notice the divisions and seemingly disjointed members. Some may even cringe to believe that the scripture above refers to the Body of Christ – the Church. However remote it may seem, the fact remains; the Word of God is true and every portion of it will be fulfilled before the return of Jesus to receive His Bride. Jesus, Himself declared:

"Heaven and earth will pass away, but My words will by no means pass away." Matthew 24:35

The restoration of Apostles now provides the vehicle for the "unity of the faith" to become a reality.

In a later chapter we will discuss the power of *"apostolic networks"* that are built relationally, which will form the operational basis for a *"united Church"*. However, in this chapter I would like us to take a closer look at Psalm 133 and some of the powerful and peculiar benefits of [46]unity.

The magnitude of the harvest that is coming to the Church of Jesus Christ in these last days can only be facilitated by a united Church. This has to be so, because of the intensity of the strain and stress that harvest brings.

There are a lot of "apostolic networks" (which will be dealt with in length in a later chapter) being formed in this season of the Church's existence and all for good reason. These are the *"nets"* that will be used to bring in the harvest of souls. However, these *"nets"* must be securely joined to handle the resulting stress from the harvest.

What type of unity will it take, to bear the strain and stress of harvest? There is a powerful contrast in the following two scriptural references which we will draw upon: Luke 5:1-7

"So it was, as the multitude pressed about Him to hear the word of God, that He stood by the Lake of Gennesaret, and saw two boats standing by the lake; but the fishermen had gone from them and were *washing their nets.* Then He got into one of the boats, which was Simon's, and asked him to put out a little from the land. And He sat down and taught the multitudes from the boat. When He had stopped speaking, He said to Simon, *"Launch out into the deep and let down your nets for a catch."* But Simon answered and said to Him, "Master,

---

[46] For more on Apostles and Church unity please see the author's book "Five Pillars of The Apostolic"; ordering details at the end of this book

we have toiled all night and caught nothing; nevertheless at Your word *I will let down the net.*" And when they had done this, *they caught a great number of fish, and their net was breaking.* So they signaled to their partners in the other boat to come and help them. And they came and filled both the boats, so that they began to sink. (Italics added)

"Then Jesus said to them, "Children, have you any food?" They answered Him, "No." And He said to them, *"Cast the net on the right side of the boat, and you will find some."* So they cast, and now they were not able to draw it in because of the multitude of fish. Therefore that disciple whom Jesus loved said to Peter, "It is the Lord!" Now when Simon Peter heard that it was the Lord, he put on his outer garment (for he had removed it), and plunged into the sea. But the other disciples came in the little boat (for they were not far from land, but about two hundred cubits), dragging the net with fish. Then, as soon as they had come to land, they saw a fire of coals there, and fish laid on it, and bread. Jesus said to them, "Bring some of the fish which you have just caught." Simon Peter went up and *dragged the net to land, full of large fish,* one hundred and fifty-three; *and although there were so many, the net was not broken."* John 21:5-11 (Italics added)

The event in the book of Luke took place prior to Jesus' resurrection, while the one in the book of John took place subsequently. I believe that the event that took place subsequent to His resurrection is a picture of what we are to expect in the end-time harvest through "apostolic networks" that have been built according to the Lord's pattern. The Lord wants us to be able to stand the stress and not break in times of increase.

There are two major things harvest or increase brings, whether in your marriage, business, ministry or whatever you are involved with and they are; tremendous weight, pressure and stress and demonic warfare; hence the reason for being united.

Remember John 17 and Jesus' prayer – He prayed for unity, the unity that is being experienced by the Godhead.

> "I do not pray for these alone, but also for those who will believe in Me through their word; *that they all may be one, as You, Father, are in Me, and I in You; that they also may be one in Us*, that the world may believe that You sent Me. And the glory which You gave Me I have given them, *that they may be one just as We are one*: I in them, and You in Me; *that they may be made perfect in one*, and that the world may know that You have sent Me, and have loved them as You have loved Me." John 17:20-23 (Italics added)

There is a tremendous anointing and grace for function whenever the Lord sees this type of unity expressed in His Body. Let us take a brief look into that powerful passage of scripture in Psalm 133:

> "Behold, how good and how pleasant it is For brethren to *dwell together in unity*! It *is like the precious oil* upon the head, Running down on the beard, The beard of Aaron, Running down on the edge of his garments. It is like the dew of Hermon, Descending upon the mountains of Zion; For there the LORD commanded the blessing— Life forevermore."

Principles And Promise Of Unity

The Principle is - dwelling together in unity or when He finds a family, or a marriage or a ministry or church, and then the promise comes.

1. Anointing - Precious oil poured on the head down to the end of the garment, an anointing will flow from God – This was a very special oil and *was not to be used on man's flesh*, however God commands it to be used wher-

ever He finds people dwelling in unity. This oil is found in Exodus 30:22-33

2. Prosperity - The dew of Hermon was higher than Zion, and it was never affected by the prevailing climate of its region. Dew is always used synonymously with blessing, favour, increase, etc – Genesis 27:27-29, Deuteronomy 33:24-29, Proverbs 19:12

3. A Blessing of life forever more, this is not just eternal life, this is something that will have generational longevity. This is building something that will become a legacy.

The Anointing Oil – Exodus 30:22-33

"Moreover the LORD spoke to Moses, saying: "Also take for yourself quality spices—five hundred shekels of liquid myrrh, half as much sweet-smelling cinnamon (two hundred and fifty shekels), two hundred and fifty shekels of sweet-smelling cane, five hundred shekels of cassia, according to the shekel of the sanctuary, and a hin of olive oil. And you shall make from these a holy anointing oil, an ointment compounded according to the art of the perfumer. It shall be a holy anointing oil. With it you shall anoint the tabernacle of meeting and the ark of the Testimony; the table and all its utensils, the lampstand and its utensils, and the altar of incense; the altar of burnt offering with all its utensils, and the laver and its base. You shall consecrate them, that they may be most holy; whatever touches them must be holy. And you shall anoint Aaron and his sons, and consecrate them, that they may minister to Me as priests. And you shall speak to the children of Israel, saying: 'This shall be a holy anointing oil to Me throughout your generations. It shall not be poured on man's flesh; nor shall you make any other like it, according to its composition. It is holy, and it shall be holy to you. Whoever compounds any like it, or whoever puts any of it on an outsider, shall be cut off from his people."

Ingredients Of The Anointing Oil

Myrrh – (Hebrew means "Bitter" or "Free") it was taken from the gum of the dwarf tree. It was supposed to flow spontaneously as the tree was cut. Pure Myrrh was bitter to the taste but had a fragrant odour. This speaks of the *suffering and the resulting anointed life and ministry* we experience. (Mark 15:23; John 19:39; Song of Solomon 3:6, 5:1-17; Matthew 2:11; Psalm 12:6; Esther 2:12; Zephaniah 3:8-9; Philippians 4:8; James 1:27; Revelation 22:1). Also note that it was used as perfume (Psalm 45:8; Proverbs 7:17; Song of Solomon 3:6), in purification rites for women (Esther 2:12), as a gift for the infant Jesus (Matthew 2:11), and in embalming (signifying death to self and the flesh) (John 19:39).

Sweet Cinnamon (Hebrew means "fragrance"). This spice comes from a small *evergreen* (constant life) tree that ha flowers with a disagreeable odour, yet the spice will improve the flavour of *bitter* substances (sweetness in suffering). See Proverbs 7:17; Psalm 104:34; 119:103; Song of Solomon 2:3; Ephesians 5:2. The *breath* is made *sweet* to prophesy. (Ezekiel 37:1-14)

Sweet-smelling Cane or Calamus (Hebrew means "to stand upright, *branch*, reed" - 1 Kings 14:15; Ezekiel 40:3; Isaiah 42:3) - It could not grow in *mire* – representing the "*flesh or sin life*". (Isaiah 19:6). This aromatic reed scents the air *while growing*. When cut down, dried, and powdered, it was used as an ingredient in the *richest* perfumes (the *fragrance of Christ* in the believer through times of crushing and shaping). (Psalm 68:30). "Branch" - the extension of the "True Vine", for the Government flows from the shoulder (Isaiah 9:6) to the Hand (Ephesians 4:11). This is His hand extended in the form of Apostles, prophets, evangelists, pastors and teachers.

Cassia (Hebrew means "stoop or bow down, scrape, *cleave*"

– *worship*). This plant has *purple* (royalty) flowers and lives at a very *high* (heavenly) altitude. *Humility* enabled by the rich anointing brings *promotion* (Proverbs 15:33). This spice was also used as incense (*worship*) and to scent garments. Christ's *regal* character manifested in us as *kings and priests unto God.* (Revelation 1:6). *"Cleave"* – Means *to become one*! - See Genesis 32:24-32; Ezekiel 27:19; Psalm 45:8; 2 Samuel 15:19-21; Joshua 23:4; Ruth 1:14-18. which were:

a. *Not To Be Poured On Man's Flesh.* The oil was for Aaron and his sons (seed) and their spiritual ministry. (Psalm 133; 104:15; 23:5)

b. *Not To Be Imitated In Any Way.* (The Harlot's Bed Of Proverbs 7:17)

c. *Not To Be Put Upon A Stranger.* The HOLY vessels of the Tabernacle are anointed (the Pentecostal experience is for the regenerated).

In spite of all the restrictions of this oil whenever the Lord sees "networking" and "unity", He responds by pouring it upon us.

CHAPTER 7

THE RESULTS OF NO BLACKSMITHS IN ISRAEL

In 1 Samuel chapter thirteen we read of a very interesting scenario which would do us well to explore and bring to light in our time. The children of Israel were at war with the Philistines, however; there were no *Blacksmiths* to be found throughout the whole land of Israel:

"Now *there was no blacksmith to be found throughout all the land of Israel*, for the Philistines said, "Lest the Hebrews make swords or spears." But all the Israelites would *go down to the Philistines to sharpen each man's ploughshare, his mattock, his ax, and his sickle*; and the charge for a sharpening was a pim for the ploughshares, the mattocks, the forks, and the axes, and to set the points of the goads. So it came about, on the day of battle, that there was neither sword nor spear found in the hand of any of the people who were with Saul and Jonathan." 1 Samuel 13:19-22 (Italics added)

In the book of Samuel we read one of the most heart wrenching and strangest stories in the Bible. The account relates to the incredible events that surrounded David's rise to the throne; in the place of Jonathan and his father Saul.

Saul represented a type of the old order or a type of the religious system of our day. David represented the future move of God, a type of the current apostolic\prophetic flow of our day. Saul represented the counterfeit [47]kingly (apostolic) anointing, while David represents the true kingly (apostolic) anointing that is alive and well, but as yet not in its rightful place.

Jonathan was born under the order of his father Saul and was mentored by that system. As a matter of fact, he was next in line for the throne. However, like so many today that are under the tutelage of the religious systems of men, Jonathan wanted something more and he knew that the true anointing rested with David.

Jonathan had vision and foresight, he prophesied of the coming kingdom in which David was anointed to rule. He loved the Davidic flow and anointing, and yet missed his true destiny simply because he could not make the break from the "*old religious order*" of his father Saul. He would not go through the process our "*Heavenly Blacksmith*" wanted to take him through!

If we are to step into all that the Lord is revealing in this hour, we had better heed the solemn warning presented to us in this incredible account. Many agree that the Lord is preparing His Church for an awesome visitation; they agree that the apostolic and prophetic is of God. Many love to be connected to this present anointing and even have it in their churches and denom-

---

[47] For more insight into this you can read the author's book "Five Pillars of the Apostolic"; ordering information at the end of this book.

inations and religious circles. However, just like Jonathan, they will miss accompanying David to the throne, if they are unable to leave the religious system of their fathers in which they have laboured. These folk will continue to hang around what God is doing; they will be content to visit with David in the wilderness and the cave Adullam, but they will not be willing to bear the reproach and step fully into what the Lord is currently doing with this *"Davidic Company"* of dissatisfied, disgruntled, distressed, discontented, debt-ridden saints.

Jonathan was an incredible individual who did some phenomenal things and still ended up missing God. Let us explore this brother's life:

1. Jonathan Was A Warrior Of The Calibre Of David

We first encounter him in *1 Samuel 13*; his father has been in power for two years and there was a major battle between the Israelites and the Philistines and the first account we read about Jonathan, was that he attacked the garrison of the Philistines (verse 3). This is very significant because for the most part, the children of Israel would run and hide from the Philistines. He attacks the Philistines on more than one occasion and on *his second attack the Lord steps in and assists him*[48].

To add to the significance of this, there were hardly any weapons in Israel at the time, for the Bible records in *verses 19 – 20* that there were no Blacksmiths (*Apostles*) to be found in Israel and that the people had to go down to the Philistines to have their swords sharpened.

> "Now there was no blacksmith to be found throughout all the land of Israel, for the Philistines said, "Lest the Hebrews make swords or spears." But all the Israelites would go down to the Philistines to sharpen each man's plowshare, his mattock, his ax, and his sickle; and the

---

[48] 1 Samuel 14:15,23

charge for a sharpening was a pim for the plowshares, the mattocks, the forks, and the axes, and to set the points of the goads. So it came about, on the day of battle, that there was neither sword nor spear found in the hand of any of the people who were with Saul and Jonathan." 1 Samuel 13:19-22

2. **He Was A Deliver Of His People** – He broke the curse of his father - 1 Samuel 14:24-30

"And the men of Israel were distressed that day, for Saul had placed the people under oath, saying, "Cursed is the man who eats any food until evening, before I have taken vengeance on my enemies." So none of the people tasted food. Now all the people of the land came to a forest; and there was honey on the ground. And when the people had come into the woods, there was the honey, dripping; but no one put his hand to his mouth, for the people feared the oath. But Jonathan had not heard his father charge the people with the oath; therefore he stretched out the end of the rod that was in his hand and dipped it in a honeycomb, and put his hand to his mouth; and his countenance brightened. Then one of the people said, "Your father strictly charged the people with an oath, saying, 'Cursed is the man who eats food this day.'" And the people were faint. But Jonathan said, "My father has troubled the land. Look now, how my countenance has brightened because I tasted a little of this honey. How much better if the people had eaten freely today of the spoil of their enemies which they found! For now would there not have been a much greater slaughter among the Philistines?"

Religion will always seek to bind you under a curse. Jesus had the same problem when He walked the face of the earth – [49]He was always rebuking "*religious*" people.

---

[49] Matthew 23 for example

3. He Stripped Himself And Gave His Kingly Robes To David

What an incredible event; what awesome selflessness. This brother had vision and was willing to lay down his call for another. 1 Samuel 18:1-4

"Now when he had finished speaking to Saul, *the soul of Jonathan was knit to the soul of David, and Jonathan loved him as his own soul.* Saul took him that day, and would not let him go home to his father's house anymore. Then Jonathan and David made a covenant, because he loved him as his own soul. *And Jonathan took off the robe that was on him and gave it to David, with his armour, even to his sword and his bow and his belt."* (Italics added)

4. He Was A Protector Of God's Anointed

David had to flee from Saul because he wanted to kill him *1 Samuel 19:1-5 and 1 Samuel 20:1-4* "Now Saul spoke to Jonathan his son and to all his servants, that they should kill David; but Jonathan, Saul's son, delighted greatly in David. So Jonathan told David, saying, "My father Saul seeks to kill you. Therefore please be on your guard until morning, and stay in a secret place and hide. And I will go out and stand beside my father in the field where you are, and I will speak with my father about you. Then what I observe, I will tell you. Thus Jonathan spoke well of David to Saul his father, and said to him, "Let not the king sin against his servant, against David, because he has not sinned against you, and because his works have been very good toward you. For he took his life in his hands and killed the Philistine, and the LORD brought about a great deliverance for all Israel. You saw it and rejoiced. Why then will you sin against innocent blood, to kill David without a cause?"… "Then David fled from Naioth in Ramah, and went and said to Jonathan, "What have I done? What is my iniquity, and what is my sin before your father, that he seeks my life?" So Jonathan said to him, "By no means! You shall not die! Indeed, my father will do nothing either great or small without first telling me. And why should my father hide this thing from me? It is not so!" Then David took an oath again, and said, "Your father certainly knows that I have found favor in your eyes, and he has said, 'Do not let Jonathan know this, lest he be grieved.' But truly, as the LORD lives and as your soul lives, there is but a step between me and death." So Jonathan said to David, "Whatever you yourself desire, I will do it for you."

Look at the men that came to David as he fled Saul *1 Samuel 22: 1-2*

"David therefore departed from there and escaped to the cave of Adullam. And when his brothers and all his father's house heard it, they went down there to him. And everyone who was in distress, everyone who was in debt, and everyone who was discontented gathered to him. So he became captain over them. And there were about four hundred men with him."

5.   He Proclaimed And Prophesied Their Destiny - 1 Samuel 23:14-18

"And David stayed in strongholds in the wilderness, and remained in the mountains in the Wilderness of Ziph. Saul sought him every day, but God did not deliver him into his hand. So David saw that Saul had come out to seek his life. And David was in the Wilderness of Ziph in a forest. Then Jonathan, Saul's son, arose and went to David in the woods and strengthened his hand in God. And he said to him, "Do not fear, for the hand of Saul my father shall not find you. You shall be king over Israel, and I shall be next to you. Even my father Saul knows that." So the two of them made a covenant before the LORD. And David stayed in the woods, and Jonathan went to his own house."

He truly had divine foresight and revelation. What an awesome announcement, as we recall that Jonathan was rightly next in line for the throne of his father. Jonathan's destiny was to sit next to David, to be his right hand man, which was his God Ordained Destiny.

Oh, this is like so many today; stuck in the *"old order"* of man's tradition; some able to proclaim the coming of something new, but not being able to enter in because of no discipline.

David steps into his Destiny. The fulfillment of his destiny begins, Glory to God, but I ask, where is Jonathan? He is dead! 1 Samuel 31:1-2 *his destiny has been denied! Why?* The answer is quite simple, he could not make the break with his religious past, and he could not break with his father. The Word of God declares:

"Do not think that I came to bring peace on earth. I did not come to bring peace but a sword. For I have come to 'set a man against his father, a daughter against her mother, and a daughter-in-law against her mother-in-law'; and 'a man's enemies will be those of his own household.' He who loves father or mother more than Me is not worthy of Me. And he who loves son or daughter more than Me is not worthy of Me. And he who does not take his cross and follow after Me is not worthy of Me. He who finds his life will lose it, and he who loses his life for My sake will find it." Matthew 10:34-39

In order to fulfill the will of God we must be constantly undergoing *transformation* – I believe it is a very relevant word for us today, let us live in that realm so that none of us end up like Jonathan and miss out on our destiny! Allow the Lord to use the Blacksmiths to sharpen and mature us. The Lord is truly reforming His Church. We are in a period of time in the earth as no other in history and as such we need to truly *"hear what the Spirit is saying to the Church in this hour"*.

The Church as we know it in the book of Acts with all five of the ministry gifts of Apostles, prophets, evangelists, pastors and teachers was a powerful, well-oiled, functioning church. However, as she went through persecution and the onslaught of roman dominance and religious indulgences she lost most if not all of her five ministry gifts given by our Lord and Saviour Jesus Christ to mature and perfect His Church. And it was not until the advent of the great reformer Martin Luther, that we saw the beginnings of the restoration of these ministry gifts to the Church.

We see the Church being launched in power in Acts 2:1-3, as the Holy Spirit descends upon the Apostles and the other saints that are gathered in the "*upper room*" on that eventful Day of Pentecost. From this point on, there are great signs, wonders and miracles arising out of a powerfully preached Christ.

The book of Acts records approximately the first thirty-five years of the Church's history from A.D 30 to 65. During this period, many souls were saved, including Paul, who became one of the more celebrated Apostles, because of his extensive contribution to the New Testament writings.

The next record we have is from the early Church fathers, recording events from about A.D 120. Subsequently, the period of the Church's history from around A.D 65 to 120 is missing.

The decline of the Church - From the records of the early Church fathers; there was a drastic deviation from the Church that was recorded in the book of Acts. The period unaccounted for has been widely accepted by Theologians and Church leaders, as the "*dark ages of the Church.*" However, it was just before his death that the Apostle Paul made this prophetic statement to the elders of the Church at Ephesus:

"And from Miletus he sent to Ephesus and called for the elders of the Church. And when they had come to him, he said to them. 'You know, from the first day that I came to Asia, in what manner I always lived among you, serving the Lord with all humility, with many tears and trials which happened to me by the plotting of the Jews; how I kept back nothing that was helpful, but proclaimed it to you, and taught you publicly and from house to house, testifying to Jews, and also to Greeks, repentance toward God and faith toward our Lord Jesus Christ. And see, now I go bound in the spirit to Jerusalem, not knowing the things that will, happen to me there, except that the Holy Spirit testifies in every city, saying that chains and tribulations await me. But none of these things move me; nor do I count my life dear to myself, so that I may finish my race with joy, and the ministry which I received from the Lord Jesus, to testify to the gospel of the grace of God. And indeed, now I know that you all, among whom I have gone preaching the kingdom of God, will see my face no more. Therefore I testify to you this day that I am innocent of the blood of all men. For I have not shunned to declare to you the whole counsel of God. *Therefore take heed to yourselves and to all the flock, among which the Holy Spirit has made you overseers, to shepherd the Church of God which He purchased with His own blood. For I know this, that after my departure savage wolves will come in among you, not sparing the flock. Also from among yourselves men will rise up, speaking perverse things, to draw away the disciples after themselves.'"* Acts 20:17-30 (Italics added)

In our study of Church history we can observe the persecution and decline of the Church. During the period between A.D 120 and A.D 315 under the Roman Empire, Christianity was outlawed and banished. Also, during that time, several edicts were passed which included orders to burn all bibles and destroy all Church buildings. From that period onward, the Church, as it was known in the book of Acts, was drastically changed and succumbed to a state of apostasy. The Church then went through a millennium of darkness, slavery and deterioration. All this was as a result of the absence of the visible functioning Blacksmiths (*Apostles*) in the Church.

CHAPTER 8

UNDERSTANDING APOSTOLIC NETWORKS

One of the rapidly growing vehicles for church growth and leadership accountability is what is referred to as "apostolic networks". In this chapter I would like to explore the different traditional avenues that exist, and are being used by those who are called into ministry; and contrast them with this new paradigm of "apostolic networking".

There exist basically three other avenues apart from "apostolic networks" in which a minister can choose to pursue his or her calling, which are:

1. The Denominational Framework:

In the truest sense, this is a well-ordered and controlled system that allows for some relationship and accountability. However, it is built on uniformity and conformity, causing it to be restrictive to any pursuit of individuality regarding vision. The concept of "*autonym*" and "*antonymous vision*" for each local church is non-existent. There is also little or no "cross pollination" with other denominations or groups. In essence, denominations can become very sectarian and can tend to resist new ideas and concepts that differ from their sometimes unique belief.

Denominationalism can sometimes resemble the tower of Babel. Please understand what I am saying here; the genesis of that tower was founded in the ideology of making a name for themselves lest they were scattered all over the face of the earth, so that they can be easily recognized and maintain their "uniqueness". It is very interesting to note that the earth at that time was of one language and one speech, so there was really no need to want an identity. It is very similar to the way the Church began on the Day of Pentecost; the Lord used the many languages that were present to speak the very same thing, and that is where the Church was born. However, at the tower of Babel, He used languages to confuse those who wanted to have their own uniformity.

"Now the whole earth had one language and one speech. And it came to pass, as they journeyed from the east, that they found a plain in the land of Shinar, and they dwelt there. Then they said to one another, "Come, let us make bricks and bake them thoroughly." They had brick for stone, and they had asphalt for mortar. And they said, "Come, let us build ourselves a city, and a tower whose top is in the heavens; let us make a name for ourselves, lest we be scattered abroad over the face of the whole earth." But the LORD came down to see the city and the tower which the sons of men had built. And the LORD said, "Indeed the people are one and they all have one language, and this is what they begin to do; now nothing that they propose to do will be withheld from them. Come, let Us go down and there confuse their language, that they may not understand one another's speech." So the LORD scattered them abroad from there over the face of all the earth, and they ceased building the city. Therefore its name is called Babel, because there the LORD confused the language of all the earth; and from there the LORD scattered them abroad over the face of all the earth." Genesis 11:1-9

Denominationalism can also be viewed as being built with *bricks*, which are made in a mould, and as such all resemble each other or are in reality the same. The concept of [50]brick making originated in Babylon and Egypt and was never intended in the construction of the House of God. In the Old Testament when King Solomon was constructing "the House for The Lord's Glory" it was done with [51]hewn out *stones*, each one having its own identity and uniqueness, but becoming a part of the whole. In the New Testament that same concept continued as the Apostle Peter so eloquently put it, concerning the building of the Church:

> "Coming to Him as to a *living stone*, rejected indeed by men, but chosen by God and precious, you also, as *living stones, are being built up a spiritual house*, a holy priest-hood, to offer up spiritual sacrifices acceptable to God through Jesus Christ." 1 Peter 2:4-5 (Italics added)

Denominations have the potential to polarize and divide the people of God, which was and still is not the Lord's intention or desire. One may ask. Can denominations change? And I would venture to say *yes*! As a matter of fact even as I write there are

---

[50] Genesis 11: 1-4 and Exodus 1:14

[51] 1 Kings 6:7

several denominations that are seeking to make the transition into becoming an *apostolic network*.

2. The Ministerial Fellowship Framework

This is basically a *"peer-level"* framework that is designed for ministers to gather and have fellowship outside the denominational grid. These ministers usually do not belong to a denomination (and even if they do, desire to see the Church united but do not know how to accomplish it, and as such think that this is a good place to begin) and are looking for relationships.

However, this framework lacks any real and solid avenue for genuine accountability. There is also a lack of vision, as there is the absence of true government and leadership. Because of the nature of this group, which sees themselves as just peers, the sense of a corporate vision and purpose is lost. Leadership is usually loose and seen merely as a facilitator or convener for the group.

This framework allows for the support of each other but only at an ethereal or superficial level as most times decisions to do so is done from the premise of "if I support the other person's venture then they will support mine as a matter of course". This kind of system invariably fails in advancing the purpose of the Lord, because it lacks corporate vision, leadership and government, thereby functioning without divine reason and intent.

3. The Independent Framework

This avenue was born out of a desire to pursue a God-given vision and mandate without oppression and intimidation that sometimes exist in the denominational framework. In this framework men and women of God have the liberty to express the vision the Lord has placed in their hearts, and not be conformed to any set mould. In essence they can maintain their individuality and autonomy. This seems good at one level but it can be very detrimental at other levels.

The detriment of this system is that it lacks any true account-ability giving occasions for leaders to become a law unto themselves, and this can prove to be very destructive. Another downside of this framework is the potential for these ministries and leaders to become isolated and cut off from the rest of the Body of Christ. The Word of God warns us of the dangers of walking alone:

"There is one alone, without companion: He has neither son nor brother. Yet there is no end to all his labors, Nor is his eye satisfied with riches. But he never asks, "For whom do I toil and deprive myself of good?" This also is vanity and a grave misfortune. Two are better than one, Because they have a good reward for their labor. For if they fall, one will lift up his companion. But woe to him who is alone when he falls, For he has no one to help him up. Again, if two lie down together, they will keep warm; But how can one be warm alone? Though one may be overpowered by another, two can withstand him. And a threefold cord is not quickly broken." Ecclesiastes 4:8-12

The Apostolic Networking Paradigm
Since the birth of the Church, on the Day of Pentecost, and its early formative years; has there been a "*Move of God*" that is dramatically changing the religious landscape. The apostolic is bringing new reforms to the Church of Jesus Christ as never before. This is the first time since the Book of Acts that we will have the Church with all [52]five ministry gifts of Apostles, prophets, evangelists, pastors and teachers functioning in her at one and the same time, awesome, just plain awesome!

Even though at the time of writing this book I am not the leader of any "apostolic network", the Lord has given me some insight into how these networks are to function. I remember one night the Lord giving me a vivid vision after which He immediately awoke me and instructed me to write down the vision. This

---

[52] Ephesians 4:11

vision contained details of an apostolic network He would cause me to function in. Much of what I am about to write, was born out of that vision.

An apostolic network can be defined as a framework that encourages individuality, and the pursuit of one's calling and vision as instructed by the Lord. However, in the midst of that pursuit of ones calling, he or she is voluntarily joined to a wider vision, based on relationship. These relationships are not synthetic, legislated nor events based, but are committed and purpose driven. It can also be described as the coming together of autonomous churches and ministries joined together by an active vision that has been released by the Lord to an appointed, gifted and functional Apostle.

Apostolic networks are not static or stereotyped as they can develop into several different forms depending on the vision and objectives of the apostolic leader. Unlike the denominational framework, in the apostolic, there is tremendous diversity and symbiotic relationships giving life and character to it. In fact, the Kingdom of God is described as a *"Net-work"* – "Once again, the kingdom of heaven is like a net..." Matthew 13:47 NIV

Networks can also be viewed as the *"Tribes of Israel"* – twelve different tribes in calling and identity, but from the very same father and comprising the entirety of all that was God-Ordained!

Defining Some Of The Functional Essentials Of Apostolic Networks:

- Every network must have a genuine, called, anointed and appointed Apostle at its helm. The revelatory gift must be at work in that Apostle, as a leader. You just cannot have an apostolic network without a genuine Apostle functioning as its leader and visionary.

- Every network has to determine the scope of its operation, as no single network would be mandated to do *all* that the Lord intends. So there must be a clear understanding of their sphere of influence and the measure of rule in that sphere. For example, Apostle Paul's mandate or *casting* was primarily to the Gentiles and that too, within specific geographical locations; while Apostle Peter's was to the Jews.

In using the parable that Jesus spoke concerning the Kingdom as a "*net*" there are several operational principles that we can deduce.

- Each apostolic network must determine its "DNA" or vision if we may. In the following passage we see that there was a careful *selection process*, they sat down and determined which was *good* – in relation to what the Lord had called those to build – versus that which was "*bad*" – did not belong to the vision or scope of what the Lord had called them to. This is very applicable for us today, as we must determine the scope of what the Lord has called us to, and not everyone will be "joined" to us. As was earlier alluded to, the Kingdom is similar to that of the twelve tribes of Israel – different identities and callings, but of the same family. Networks are going to have to function in like manner, knowing what is their "DNA" or "tribe".

"Once again, the kingdom of heaven is like a net that was let down into the lake and caught all kinds of fish. When it was full, the fishermen pulled it up on the shore. Then they sat down and collected the good fish in baskets, but threw the bad away." Matthew 13:47-48 NIV

"After these things Jesus showed Himself again to the disciples at the Sea of Tiberias, and in this way

He showed Himself: Simon Peter, Thomas called the Twin, Nathanael of Cana in Galilee, the sons of Zebedee, and two others of His disciples were together. Simon Peter said to them, "I am going fishing." They said to him, "We are going with you also." They went out and immediately got into the boat, *and that night they caught nothing.* But when the morning had now come, Jesus stood on the shore; yet the disciples did not know that it was Jesus. Then Jesus said to them, "Children, have you any food?" They answered Him, "No." And He said to them, *"Cast the net on the right side of the boat*, and you will find some." *So they cast, and now they were not able to draw it in because of the multitude of fish."* John 21:1-6 (Italics added)

• In the passage of scripture above, referred to from the book of John, we see the importance of each network knowing the scope of its casting. Here we see Peter (the apostolic head of that *"network"*) determining where they would cast their nets. They obviously did so in the wrong direction and Jesus had to adjust their vision by instructing them to make a casting on the other side, resulting in increase.

We have to understand that there will be some networks called to specific "people groups", ([53]for example the Apostles Paul and Peter) some to specific nations, some to even specific professions and the list can go on. Each network must know its operational scope and mandate.

Networks will also have to be maintained, as they deal with the stress and strain of relationships. In the following scriptural references we would look at areas of maintenance:

[53] Galatians 2:7-8

- The washing of the net. This is also vital for the operations within the network; there will be times when the "*net*" has to be washed. Without this periodic cleansing the casting can be accurate in terms of its location but there could be a wrong catch for one reason or the other. So there is the dimension of throwing the "*bad*" but there is also the dimension of "*washing*" the net.

"So it was, as the multitude pressed about Him to hear the word of God, that He stood by the Lake of Gennesaret, and saw two boats standing by the lake; but the fishermen had gone from them and *were washing their nets*. Luke 5:1-2 (Italics added)

- The *mending* of the net. There are times when the stress and strain of relationship will test the integrity of the net and it may snap or break. This is not to be viewed as a sign of disunity or the end of a network. The Apostles [54]Paul and Barnabus had their "differences" but that did not stop the work from progressing. Similarly with the Apostles [55]Paul and Peter, just to cite a couple of situations within "*apostolic networks*" where there was a need for *mending* as happened in both cases.

"Going on from there, He saw two other brothers, James the son of Zebedee, and John his brother, in the boat with Zebedee their father, *mending their nets*. And He called them…" Matthew 4:21 (Italics added)

Mending spoken of here is derived from the Greek word "Katartismos" and conveys the following meaning: To establish to an already determined standard, to perfect and also to equip. This is very word that is used in Ephesians 4:11-12 when it says – "And He Himself gave

---

some to be apostles, some prophets, some evangelists, and some pastors and teachers, 12 for the *equipping* of the saints for the work of ministry, for the edifying of the body of Christ..."

Because each network should be born out of a clear vision, standard and mandate from the Lord, *if "break-age"* occurs, mending is easy and achievable. There already exists a predetermined standard to work towards.

Even though provisions are made in the event of *"break-age"*, it is quite possible to build a network without it. Again, using the example of *"the net"* Jesus used in speaking about the Kingdom, we see in the following example of a very large catch without any breakage to the *"net"*. "But the other disciples came in the little boat (for they were not far from land, but about two hundred cubits), dragging the net with fish. Then, as soon as they had come to land, they saw a fire of coals there, and fish laid on it, and bread. Jesus said to them, "Bring some of the fish which you have just caught." Simon Peter went up and dragged the net to land, full of large fish, one hundred and fifty-three; and *although there were so many, the net was not broken.* John 21:8-11 (Italics added)

There is what can be called *"cross-pollination"* between networks as seen in Peter calling the men from another boat to come and help them, causing the framework for true unity to be put in place.

"When He had stopped speaking, He said to Simon, "Launch out into the deep and let down your nets for a catch." But Simon answered and said to Him, "Master, we have toiled all night and caught nothing; nevertheless at Your word I will let down the net." And when they had done this, *they caught a great number of fish, and their net was breaking.* So they signaled *to their partners in the other boat to come and help them.* And they came and *filled both the boats,* so that they began to sink." Luke 5:4-7 (Italics added)

We are going to see this networking concept of the Kingdom of God expand in this season, as this is going to be the framework for accurate expansion of the Kingdom of God in the earth. Networks are going to relate with each other and we will see the coming together of the Body of Christ like never before. The Blacksmiths/Apostles are being restored and are being released to function alongside the prophets, evangelists, pastors and teachers in building an awesome Church in the earth.

Benefits Of Apostolic Networking
As we see the emergence of genuine apostolic networks there will undoubtedly be benefits that we would all enjoy. These benefits will include:

- Relationships that will not rob us of our call and vision in the Lord.

- Accountability that will be relationally based, rather than control based.

- Greater productivity and accuracy in the things that the Lord has assigned us to.

- Tapping into the "wisdom base" that is given to Apostles. Apostles are referred to as "[56]*wise master builders*". Apostles are also referred to as "*wise men*" by Jesus Himself as recorded in the following:

  "Therefore the wisdom of God also said, 'I will send them prophets and *apostles*, and some of them they will kill and persecute…" Luke 11:49 (Italics added)

  "Therefore, indeed, I send you prophets, *wise men,*

---
[56] 1 Corinthians 3:10

and scribes: some of them you will kill and crucify, and some of them you will scourge in your synagogues and persecute from city to city..." Matthew 23:34 (Italics added)

- Tapping into Divine Revelation and Grace that is released to Apostles: Paul puts it beautifully in the following verses of scripture:

"For this reason I, Paul, the prisoner of Christ Jesus for you Gentiles—if indeed you have heard of the *dispensation of the grace* of God which *was given to me for you,* how that *by revelation He made known to me the mystery* (as I have briefly written already, by which, when you read, you *may understand my knowledge in the mystery of Christ*), which in other ages *was not made known to the sons of men,* as it has *now been revealed by the Spirit to His holy apostles and prophets*: that the Gentiles should be fellow heirs, of the same body, and partakers of His promise in Christ through the gospel, of which I *became a minister according to the gift of the grace of God given to me* by the effective working of His power. To me, who am less than the least of all the saints, *this grace was given,* that I should preach among the Gentiles the unsearchable riches of Christ, and to make all see what is the fellowship of the mystery, which from the beginning of the ages has been hidden in God who created all things through Jesus Christ; to the intent that now the manifold wisdom of God might be made known by the church to the principalities and powers in the heavenly places, according to the eternal purpose which He accomplished in Christ Jesus our Lord..." Ephesians 3:1-11 (Italics added)

- Enhancement of Divine Order and Governmental Strength in the network churches. When Apostle Paul established ministries in Crete, he later sent Titus to establish

"Divine Order and Governmental Structure" for their proper functioning:

> "For this reason I left you in Crete, that you should set in order the things that are lacking, and appoint elders in every city as I commanded you…" Titus 1:5

One of the key and pivotal things that the Lord is now doing through the apostolic and apostolic network of churches that He is raising up; is the reforming of government. For too long churches have been run by "deacon boards" and systems that rob the quality of life from the visionaries of the church. The Bible is quite clear as to the governmental structure that is to exist within the church:

> "And God has *appointed* these in the church: *first apostles*, *second prophets*, *third teachers*, after that miracles, then gifts of healings, helps, administrations, varieties of tongues." 1 Corinthians 12:28 (Italics added)

The Word of God declares that God has *"appointed"* (set with permanence) in the Church – *first* – *Apostles*! This must be the priority in the Church; Apostles and the apostolic must be first set. This must be foundational in the church and the order continues from there. When the proper governmental structure is put in place, I dare say that we are going to see more of God's power released in and through the Church. It is first Apostles, second prophets, third teachers (encompassing the evangelist and pastor), and *after that*, we can see miracles and gifts of healings flowing in abundance.

The apostolic must be first, as it has the anointing and capacity for breakthrough. It has the power to bring change and reformation.

Defining Apostolic Relationships
In this section we will seek to bring some clarity and defini-

tion to *"apostolic relationships"* and how we access the apostolic within the local church community.

There exist three ways that local churches can access the apostolic but before we go into them let me first make this very important statement:

You can seek to activate and desire to have an operation or manifestation of a spiritual gift without capturing, walking or moving in the relevant move of God that is producing that manifestation or gift. For example; you can receive or even *"prophesy"* but not become *"prophetic"*. In like manner, one can receive information about the apostolic, but never embrace and walk in the apostolic. This has been the problem with the church for centuries – we get all this information, but the corresponding walk to match the talk is lacking. In this hour, the Lord is truly releasing the technology for us to walk in what is being released as we tap into this "apostolic dimension".

Let us now seek to identify and clarify the three ways that the apostolic can be accessed:

First Of All There Is The Resident Apostle!
This is existent in the local church that was founded by an Apostle and who permanently resides in that church. Or there is in that local church recognized, identifiable, ordained and appointed Apostles. For example the church at Antioch:

> "Now in the church that was at Antioch there were certain prophets and teachers: Barnabas, Simeon who was called Niger, Lucius of Cyrene, Manaen who had been brought up with Herod the tetrarch, and Saul. As they ministered to the Lord and fasted, the Holy Spirit said, "Now separate to Me Barnabas and Saul for the work to which I have called them." Then, having fasted and prayed, and laid hands on them, they sent them away." Acts 13:1-3

This church was functioning on proper governmental structure and order. There were certainly Apostles in it, as it was founded by the Apostles. As mentioned earlier, Barnabus was a recognized, ordained and appointed Apostle and also Paul (Saul). They had the order correct - Apostles, prophets and teachers, and it was from that "order" the Holy spirit spoke and gave "apostolic commissioning" to Barnabus and Paul (Saul).

Another example was the church at Jerusalem, which had several Apostles residing in it, as was evidenced when the Holy Spirit brought a scattering to the Believers in that church:

> "At that time a great persecution arose against *the church which was at Jerusalem*; and *they were all scattered* throughout the regions of Judea and Samaria, *except the apostles*. Acts 8:1 (Italics added)

Secondly There Is The Trans-Local/Transitory Apostle!

This type of relationship is for those local churches that do not have a resident Apostle. They would receive from an apostolic source through, sometimes unscheduled visits. In this way they can have the benefits of apostolic ministry even though they do not have resident Apostles in their church.

Thirdly There Is The Networking Or Relational Apostle!

This is the dimension of relationship where you have a network of churches built on relationship drawing from the *apostolic source* of that network.

Apostolic Source

The term *apostolic source* is referred to the place, a local church, church leadership or the Believer receives the needed input of the apostolic. Since the church is built or is being built upon the foundation that is laid by Apostles and prophets, it is essential that all churches have an apostolic source; either resident, transitory or through its relationship in an apostolic network.

Point to consider. Those who are called to be Apostles and to be the apostolic leader of a network of churches, while they themselves need relationships, they do not necessarily *need a head or man covering them*. This is very important, as many would ask *"who is your covering"* or *"who is your Apostle"*? All Apostles, because of the nature of the calling and gifting, *MUST* be connected to heaven. While they would relate to others, and that is very vital and necessary, their primary source *MUST* be heaven.

The point that is being made is this – not everyone that functions under an apostolic anointing is an Apostle. In many regions of the earth, with specific emphasis to North America if you were to throw a stone out of a window into the street below, there are significant odds that you will hit an Apostle. Today, almost everyone is an Apostle. Some cannot even correctly spell the word, but have it on their "calling cards". However, as we understand it with every move of God's Holy Spirit to bring reformation and adjustment to the church, there have been, and will continue to be, excesses in the process. It was no different in the great Pentecostal move, where several individuals died as a result of drinking poison and being bitten by venomous snakes, all because of incorrect perception and application of one of the scriptural texts that came alive during that move, which was:

"And these signs will follow those who believe: In My name they will cast out demons; they will speak with new tongues; they will take up serpents; and if they drink anything deadly, it will by no means hurt them; they will lay hands on the sick, and they will recover." Mark 16:17-18

Understanding Apostolic Relationships
As was said earlier there are basically three dimensions of *"apostolic relationships"*, which are "Resident, Transitory/Temporary (making brief visits into a region or place) and Networking"; but how do these relationships work?

Apostolic relationships are built and function on several levels. There is what can be referred to as *"Apostolic Doctrine"* as was declared in:

"Then those who gladly received his word were baptized; and that day about three thousand souls were added to them. And *they continued steadfastly in the apostles' doctrine and fellowship*, in the breaking of bread, and in prayers. Acts 2:41-42 (Italics added)

There are several things that can be deduced from the above text:

a.) There is something called *"the Apostles' doctrine"* and it was vital for the early church and continues to be vital for the 21st Century Church. The *"Apostles' doctrine"* can be referred to as the Apostles' teaching, instructions, impartation, system of belief or life style.

b.) That relationships were built *"apostolically"* by the believers *continuing steadfastly* in the "A*postles' doctrine"*. The Church was being built and still continues to be built upon the foundation of "Apostles and prophets" – the revelation of Jesus Christ that is being released by these foundational ministries. The terminology *"continued steadfastly"* is derived from theGreek [57]*pros kartereo* with its meaning rendered - "to be strong towards" (pros - "towards," used intensively, and kartereo - "to be strong"), "to endure in, or persevere in, to be continually steadfast with a person or thing," is used of "continuing" in prayer with others, Acts 1:14; Rom 12:12; Col 4:2; in the Apostles' teaching/doctrine, Acts 2:42; in the Temple, 2:46 ("continuing steadfastly," RV). It is also translated – to give unremitting care and attention to, to persevere, not loosing heart or becoming faint; to give one's undivided, attention to someone or

---

[57] From Vine's Expository Dictionary of Biblical Words, Copyright (c)1985, Thomas Nelson Publishers

something, to be devoted. Steadfastness is one of the identifiable qualities of apostles and apostolic minded people. There is just "no quit" in them. Built into the very core and foundation of the apostolic, is the ability to press through and breakthrough tremendous odds, hence the reason we need that *"proton"* (first) anointing in any-thing we seek to accomplish for the Lord.

c.) The other salient point that can be derived from Acts 2:42 is the whole dynamic of *"apostolic fellowship"*. The word used for fellowship is the Greek *"koinonia"* and is rendered - "communion, fellowship, sharing in common" (from koinos, "common"), is translated "com-munion" in 1 Corinthians 10:16; Philemon 6, RV, "fel-lowship," for KJV, "communication"; it is most frequent-ly translated "fellowship"; (b) "that which is the outcome of fellowship, a contribution." To give the right hand of fellowship as a pledge of covenantal relationship and friendship were all part of what was deemed "apostolic fellowship". There is also another Greek word that is translated fellowship, which is koinonos and denotes "a partaker" or "partner" in 1 Corinthians 10:20 it is used with ginomai, "to become," "that ye should have com-munion with," RV (KJV, fellowship with).

Another level of apostolic relationships is built through what can be described as *"apostolic imitation"*. We can draw this from the Apostle Paul's position in the following texts:

"Imitate me, just as I also imitate Christ. Now I praise you, brethren, that you remember me in all things and keep the traditions just as I delivered them to you. 1 Corinthians 11:1-2 (Italics added)

"I do not write these things to shame you, but as my beloved children I warn you. For though you might have ten thousand instructors in Christ, yet you do not have many fathers; for in Christ Jesus I have begotten you through the gospel. Therefore *I urge you, imitate* me. For this reason I have sent Timothy to you, who is my beloved and faithful son in the Lord, *who will remind you of my ways in Christ, as I teach everywhere in every church.*" 1 Corinthians 4:14-17 (Italics added)

Imitate is derived from the Greek "*mimeomai*", which is used as the verb and is rendered - "a mimic, an actor" (English, "mime," etc.), is always translated "to imitate" in the RV, for KJV, "to follow," (a) of imitating the conduct of missionaries/Apostles, 2 Thessalonians 3:7,9; the faith of spiritual guides, Hebrews 13:7; (b) that which is good, 3 John 11. The verb is always used in exhortations, and always in the continuous tense, suggesting a constant habit or practice.

The noun is "*mimetes*", and is rendered – "an imitator," so the RV for KJV, "follower," is always used in a good sense in the NT. In 1 Corinthians 4:16; 11:1; Ephesians 5:1; Hebrews 6:12, it is used in exhortations, accompanied by the verb "*ginomai*" - "to be, or to become," and in the continuous tense, except in Hebrews 6:12, where the aorist or momentary tense indicates a decisive act with permanent results. In 1 Thessalonians 1:6; 2:14, the accompanying verb is in the aorist tense, referring to the definite act of conversion in the past. These instances, coupled with the continuous tenses referred to, teach that what we became at conversion we must diligently continue to be thereafter.

As seen from the Greek understanding of this word "*imitate*" we are to continue diligently in what we see the Apostles doing and living. We cannot be imitators of someone who no longer exist; hence we need to have Apostles around from start to finish, when the church comes to full maturity for function in the earth.

Oh, this is so powerful! Part of the operational technology that Apostles function from, is the ability to father [or mother] others in the Lord. A son or daughter in the Lord follows or imitates their father because it is their DNA, it's in their genes. There is a huge difference between an instructor, who may be able to teach us "principles for success" and a father who can birth us in the things of God.

Today we see a lot of "*apostolic emulators*" and not "*apostolic imitators*" and the Lord wants us to return to the dimension of "*imitators*" of the Apostles. The word emulate is derived from the Greek word used for emulation – "zelos, parazeloo" In Galatians 5:20 of the King James Version it is the translation of zelos ("zeal," "earnestness," "enthusiasm") where it is classed among "the works of the flesh" and signifies the stirring up of jealousy or envy in others, because of what we are, or have, or profess. In the Merriam-Webster's Collegiate Dictionary it is stated that "emulate" means – to strive to equal or excel. Another translation renders it "the copycatting" of that which is perceived as successful so that one can be elevated or perceived to be successful. However we look at it, emulation is wrong and sinful as far as the Lord is concerned. However, He encourages us to be "*apostolic imitators*"; and followers of that, which is good; thereby releasing the apostolic dimension throughout the Church and not just the personality of a man or woman.

In reality, what is being expressed is that we are to be imitators of the example set by the Apostles. We are to be imitators of the "apostolic life" and not the personality or charisma of an individual. The anointing and grace gift of the apostolic that the Lord has placed within that individual's life that is what we are to imitate. As we do this, we will be building "apostolic relationship" and also be partakers of what can be best described as "*apostolic grace*", which is another level in the "apostolic relationship" process and outworking.

Apostolic grace is that quality of grace that is released by the Lord upon Apostles. It is a powerful dimension of grace so that they can effectively fulfill all the Will of God. In many of his writings to the churches, the Apostle Paul used the term "grace to you[58]" at the onset of these letters. It is also found in the Apostle Peter's letter[59] and the Apostle John's letter[60] to the churches in the book of Revelation.

As one partakes of this "apostolic grace", through "apostolic relationships", what are some of the benefits? As we re-visit some of the letters that the Apostles wrote to those who were in their "network of churches" we will see some of the benefits of this "apostolic grace".

- Powerful prayer support[61]

- The power to finish or complete[62]. This is a powerful dimension of the apostolic anointing and one of the reasons that the Lord now restores this gift back to His Church. I believe that we are living in the last days and the church needs an anointing to *"finish"* and to do it with strength and style; not in cowardly fashion. Part of the technology that the Lord has graced apostles with, is the ability to endure and win against great odds. The Early Church was birthed through great opposition, persecution and great odds, but still grew and multiplied at an alarming rate. The ability *to finish* is definitely part of the blessings that comes from *"apostolic relationship"*. I prophetically declare to you, that it will be even greater in these last days as the Lord fully restores His Apostles, with a *"finishing anointing and mentality"* to His Church. *Hallelujah!*

- The power that comes from *"apostolic joinings"* as described by the Apostle Paul in his letter to the

---

[58] Romans 1:7, 1 Corinthians 1:3, 2 Corinthians 1:2, Galatians 1:3, Ephesians 1:2, Philippians 1:2, Colossians 1:2, 1 Thessalonians 1:1, 2 Thessalonians 1:2

[59] 1 Peter 1:2

[60] Revelation 1:4

[61] Romans 1:9, Philippians 1:4, Colossians 1:3, 1 Thessalonians 1:2

[62] Philippians 1:6

Philippian church when he was in chains and bonds:

"… just as it is right for me *to think this of you* all, *because I have you in my heart*, inasmuch as both in my chains and in the defense and confirmation of the gospel, *you all are partakers with me of grace.* For God is my witness, *how greatly I long for you all* with the affection of Jesus Christ." Philippians 1:7-8

This is truly another powerful dimension of "apostolic grace" that comes through relationship. Here we see the Apostle Paul in chains and bonds and all he can think and pray about are the saints that he is undoubtedly connected to. This is true "apostolic relationship". This is the dimension that the Lord wants returned to His Church through the current "apostolic reformation" that is taking place in the Church. Because the Church was in the Apostle's heart there was a release of "apostolic grace". Awesome!

• Another dynamic that this "apostolic grace" produces is that of "*mutual love*" that enhances true "apostolic relationships". It is not the type of one-sided deference we see in some apostolic circles and networks, where some almost border on the worshipping of "their Apostle". This is love that is mutual as described in the following:

"For God is my witness, *how greatly I long for you all with the affection of Jesus Christ. And this I pray, that your love may abound still more and more* in knowledge and all discernment, that you may approve the things that are excellent, that you may be sincere and without offense till the day of Christ, being filled with the fruits of righteousness which are by Jesus Christ, to the glory and praise of God." Philippians 1:8-11

This "mutual love" spoken of is not the "*sluppyaguppy*"

type of love that we see masquerading itself as genuine, agape love. No, this is the genuine thing and finds itself abounding in knowledge and discernment. Again, this is another undeniable dimension of apostolic knowledge and discernment, and the Apostle Paul released that through his "apostolic grace" to the churches and Saints of his "apostolic network".

Further Essentials For Apostolic Networks
In the book of Matthew as Jesus sent out His Apostles to accomplish some assignments, there are some powerful principles for apostolic networks to function on:

"These twelve Jesus sent out and commanded them, saying: "Do not go into the way of the Gentiles, and do not enter a city of the Samaritans. But go rather to the lost sheep of the house of Israel. And as you go, preach, saying, 'The kingdom of heaven is at hand.' "Heal the sick, cleanse the lepers, raise the dead, cast out demons. Freely you have received, freely give. Provide neither gold nor silver nor copper in your money belts, nor bag for your journey, nor two tunics, nor sandals, nor staffs; for a worker is worthy of his food. Now whatever city or town you enter, inquire who in it is worthy, and stay there till you go out. And when you go into a household, greet it. If the household is worthy, let your peace come upon it. But if it is not worthy, let your peace return to you. And whoever will not receive you nor hear your words, when you depart from that house or city, shake off the dust from your feet. Assuredly, I say to you, it will be more tolerable for the land of Sodom and Gomorrah in the day of judgment than for that city!" "Behold, I send you out as sheep in the midst of wolves. Therefore be wise as serpents and harmless as doves. But beware of men, for they will deliver you up to councils and scourge you in their synagogues. You will be brought before governors and kings for My sake, as a testimony to them and to the

Gentiles. But when they deliver you up, do not worry about how or what you should speak. For it will be given to you in that hour what you should speak; for it is not you who speak, but the Spirit of your Father who speaks in you. Now brother will deliver up brother to death, and a father his child; and children will rise up against parents and cause them to be put to death. And you will be hated by all for My name's sake. But he who endures to the end will be saved. When they persecute you in this city, flee to another. For assuredly, I say to you, you will not have gone through the cities of Israel before the Son of Man comes. A disciple is not above his teacher, nor a servant above his master. It is enough for a disciple that he be like his teacher, and a servant like his master. If they have called the master of the house Beelzebub, how much more will they call those of his household! Therefore do not fear them. For there is nothing covered that will not be revealed, and hidden that will not be known." Matthew 10: 5-26

Apostolic Principles:
1. In verses 5-6 the Apostles are given *"very clear directions"*. From this we can glean that Apostles and apostolic networks must be given a specific mandate and vision. This also reveals to us that there is specific *"casting"* for every network. Not everyone will be called to do the same thing. As I stated earlier, it is like the Apostle Paul's network that was specifically sent to work among the gentiles, versus the Apostle Peter's network that was mandated to work primarily among the Jews. Every network must know their specific call and casting. Please understand that there are specific spheres of operation for every apostolic network. Part of the operational dynamic of Apostles is in knowing his/her sphere of influence and authority. Not knowing this, often times could be the detriment of many, as they step outside of their allotted grace for the sphere the Lord has assigned them to. This is clearly shown in the Apostle Paul's writ-

ing to the Corinthian church, in which he states:

"We, however, will not boast beyond measure, but within the limits of the sphere which God appointed us—a sphere which especially includes you. For we are not overextending ourselves (as though our authority did not extend to you), for it was to you that we came with the gospel of Christ; not boasting of things beyond measure, that is, in other men's labors, but having hope, that as your faith is increased, we shall be greatly enlarged by you in our sphere, to preach the gospel in the regions beyond you, and not to boast in another man's sphere of accomplishment." 2 Corinthians 10:13-16

Apostolic spheres are very clear, and this is one area that all apostolic networks must be absolutely certain about, as this will minimize the conflict and unnecessary pressure that can result from a lack of understanding this vital principle. Once again we hear the Apostle Paul's claim as he spoke to the Corinthian church: *"Am I not an apostle? Am I not free? Have I not seen Jesus Christ our Lord? Are you not my work in the Lord? If I am not an apostle to others, yet doubtless I am to you* [implying that if he did not have any other sphere of influence, he undoubtedly had among them, the Corinthian church]. For you are the seal of my apostleship in the Lord. 1 Corinthians 9:1-2 (Italics and Parenthesis added)

2. In verse 7 they are instructed to preach *"the Kingdom."* There must be a relevant Kingdom message preached by the Apostles in this time. There must be that strong Kingdom focus. Even though apostolic networks will have specific mandates and castings they must always see the broader picture, which is Kingdom. All that we do, is designed to cause His Kingdom to come and His Will to be done on earth as it is in heaven.

3. In verse 8 *"miracles, signs and wonders"* are to be accomplished by the Apostles. This dimension has been the cause of much debate among apostolic people as some say that you can be an Apostle and not see this dimension in your life and ministry. However in this writing I want to view this from the perspective of apostolic networks, and as such, I believe that in apostolic networks there would be this dimension functioning. Also, I would prefer to err on the side of believing the Lord for this to be active and existent in an Apostle. The Apostle Paul made a very interesting statement in the following text: "I have become a fool in boasting; you have compelled me. For I ought to have been commended by you; *for in nothing was I behind the most eminent apostles,* though I am nothing. *Truly the signs of an apostle were accomplished among you with all perseverance, in signs and wonders and mighty deeds."* 2 Corinthians 12:11-12 (Italics added). It would seem to suggest that the Apostle Paul was in fact ascribing this dimension to all eminent Apostles.

4. Whenever God gives vision, *provision is made*. In verses 9-10 promise of provision is made. This is another tremendous promise for the apostolic – a total release of resource. The very word *"resource"* has an extremely powerful foundation. This word was derived from the French *ressource,* a derivative from the Old French *ressourse* which means - relief, resource, from *resourdre* to relieve, literally, to rise again, from Latin *resurgere* – which is translated *resurrection!* Now that is powerful. There will be times apostolic networks will experience, as it were, a resurrection in terms of accomplishing the tasks that the Lord has assigned them to.

5. The apostolic is committed to that *which is worthy*. In verse 11-13 careful inquiries are to be made for that which is worthy. This is a major strategy in building

apostolic networks in this hour. Because the true nature of apostolic networks must be built relationally, the Lord gives the framework for function in any territory that He sends. He commands that the first thing we do is to seek for *"who is worthy"* and build a relationship there. As a matter of fact, He actually said to look for a "household", implying family relationships exist. The word for household used is the Greek "oikos" and is rendered family. It is from that frame work we can then effectively take that region or territory. In essence you are to look for *"the son/daughter of peace"* and from that place, function. Please understand that the "oikos" can also mean "a local church family". Whether it is a natural or spiritual family one thing is certain; the apostolic is not to attach itself to that which is unworthy. It must remain pure by attaching itself to that which is worthy.

6. In verses 14-15 the Lord promises that any *refusal of the Apostles' Kingdom message* will end in disaster.

7. The Lord releases *divine wisdom* as He sends out the Apostles, verse 16. Wisdom is another powerful defining characteristic of the apostolic, and you can read more on this powerful dimension in my book *"Five Pillars of The Apostolic"*[63]. An apostolic network just *cannot* be effective without this important grace gift from the Lord. Every apostolic network must know how to tap in and access this dimension, if not they will be doomed to failure before they even begin. Wisdom is profitable to direct, it is wisdom that builds the house. The apostle Paul declared that Apostles are called to be *"wise master builders"*. If apostolic networks are to be all that the Lord intends, they will have to build wisely for the Lord. Remember, the Apostle James declared this to us: "If any of you lacks wisdom, let him ask of God, who gives to

---

[63] Ordering details at the end of this book

all liberally and without reproach, and it will be given to him. But let him ask in faith, with no doubting, for he who doubts is like a wave of the sea driven and tossed by the wind." James 1:5-6

8. In verses 17-18; 21-23 the Lord warns them about *persecutions*, declaring that it cannot be avoided.

9. Apostles are given *divine revelation*, as promised in verse 19-20; 26-27. This is another key dimension of the apostolic; the ability to decode the mysteries of the Lord. Mysteries that are locked up in the Word of God are accessed through "divine revelation" and this is part of the operating technology that can be accessed by apostles. Again we can site the Apostle Paul's declaration of this:

"For this reason I, Paul, the prisoner of Christ Jesus for you Gentiles—if indeed you have heard of the dispensation of the grace of God which was given to me for you, *how that by revelation He made known to me the mystery* (as I have briefly written already, by which, when you read, *you may understand my knowledge in the mystery of Christ*), which in other ages was not made known to the sons of men, as it has now been revealed by the Spirit to His holy apostles and prophets:" Ephesians 3:1-5 (Italics added)

"I now rejoice in my sufferings for you, and fill up in my flesh what is lacking in the afflictions of Christ, for the sake of His body, which is the church, of which *I became a minister according to the stewardship from God which was given to me for you*, to fulfill the word of God, *the mystery which has been hidden from ages and from generations, but now has been revealed to His saints*. To them God willed to make known what are the riches of the glory of this mystery among the

Gentiles: which is Christ in you, the hope of glory."
Colossians 1:24-27 (Italics added)

10. Verses 24-25 *identify the Apostles with their source*, from the perspective that they should be encouraged, and not lose heart because of any adverse situation. This is the power of the apostolic – even though you would relate to others, there must be that connection from heaven, your true apostolic source, and every apostolic network must experience this.

11. Luke 11:28 makes this statement - "for which of you, intending to build a tower, does not sit down first and count the cost, whether he has enough to finish it." We see this same dynamics of a *apostolic cost*, in verses 34-39. The *"finishing anointing"* is another powerful dimension of the apostolic. Apostolic networks must be built on the premise that they will accomplish all that the Lord has ordained for them. They must be able to say, like the Apostle Paul, at the end of the road: "I have fought the good fight, I have finished the race, I have kept the faith." 2 Timothy 4:7. In the light of this it is advisable that the cost be counted before stepping into "apostolic ministry" as it may not add up to be all that some are making it. This is so because in some quarters, people are making the apostolic what the Lord never intended it to be and we all know that with every move of God's Holy Spirit in bringing reformation and restoration, there has been and will continue to be, excess and misinformation resulting in people being hurt and disillusioned.

12. Verses 40-42 speak about *"apostolic reward"*, declaring that there are tremendous blessings and rewards in receiving the Apostles. In the same way the Word of God declares that if we receive a prophet in the name of a

prophet we will receive "a prophet's reward[64]" it is no different with the apostolic. There are tremendous benefits in receiving apostolic ministry some of which was detailed in an earlier section.

Remember the Word of our Lord, Jesus Christ as He admonished and encouraged us:

"He who receives you receives Me, and he who receives Me receives Him who sent Me. *He who receives a prophet* [Apostle, evangelist, pastor, and teacher] *in the name of a prophet* [Apostle, evangelist, pastor, and teacher] *shall receive a prophet's* [an Apostle's, evangelist's, a pastor's, or a teacher's] *reward.* And he who receives a righteous man in the name of a righteous man shall receive a righteous man's reward. Matthew 10:40-41 (Italics and Parenthesis added).

---

[64] Matthew 10:41

Other Titles By The Author

Five Pillars Of The Apostolic

Towards A Mature Church

Discerning seasons and times is such an important task in the day that we live. If, as the body of the LORD we fail to do so, we will fail in expressing the heart of Father God. It has become very evident that a new day has dawned in the earth, as the Lord restores the foundational ministry of the Apostle back to His Church. There is an awesome, powerful, militant church rising in the earth, as Apostles are being restored to take their place alongside the prophets, evangelists, pastors and teachers to bring the Church into unity and to a place of maturity for function in the earth. It is indeed a glorious time to be alive and be connected to the purpose of the Lord.

The body of Christ truly is reaching unprecedented levels of power, revelation, and effectiveness. Michael Scantlebury is a keen observer of this historic transition and the key role that apostles are playing in it. Five Pillars of the Apostolic has my recommendation. **C. Peter Wagner, Chancellor,** Wagner Leadership Institute

The 21st century has exploded in apostolic revelation and understanding... I highly recommend this book not only to church leaders but to lay people everywhere... **Apostle Emanuele Cannistraci** Apostolic Leader of Apostolic Missions International San Jose, California, USA

This book provides an excellent tool for the Church to measure apostolic claims by the yardstick of the author's five-pillars of apostolic grace... **Dr. Roger W. Sapp** All Nations Ministries Southlake, Texas, USA

Rooted firmly in biblical teachings this book is a "must" for all leaders who desire to keep their Churches on the cutting edge... **Pastor Ajith Abeyratne** Senior Pastor, Calvary Church Mirihana, Sri Lanka

Apostolic Purity

*In Pursuit of **His** Excellence*

A Sequel to Five Pillars of The Apostolic

In every dispensation, in every move of God's Holy Spirit to bring restoration and reformation to His Church, righteousness, holiness and purity has always been of utmost importance to the Lord. And it is no different in the current move of God that is bringing apostolic restoration to His Church. In many places, the people of God are crying out for His Manifested Presence. Fed-up with mere programs, activities and shallow religious works, saints from every nation are storming heaven and proclaiming that the *Glory of God* must cover the earth, as the waters cover the sea.

There is a purifying that has already begun in the ranks of professing Christianity. Some apostles in training are being cast into the backsides of the desert to be purified. Others are being purified in motion, they are in charge of networks and ministries, but there is a deep inner work being done. Still, others are being purified under the *"Saul and Laban types of ministries"* – Saul took the best from the people and Laban deceived Jacob into working longer for him before receiving his legitimate inheritance. However, the Father chooses to do it, it is being done, so that the earth can see His Glory through the Church.

Kingdom Advancing Prayer - Volumes I & II

Part of the technology that is being released into the Church as the Lord restores Apostles, is what we describe as Kingdom Advancing Prayer. This kind of prayer puts the Kingdom of God first and foremost; it is above any personal need or agenda. It is similar to the kind of prayer that Elijah prayed, as the Lord used him to turn a whole nation around, and destroy the demonic influence that threatened to thwart the Lord's purpose. It is reflective of the prayer that Jesus prayed as He prepared to bring to completion His Father's will and go to the cross.

The Church of Jesus Christ is stronger and much more determined and equipped than she has ever been, and strong, aggressive, powerful, Spirit-Filled, Kingdom-centred prayers are being lifted in every nation in the earth. We are seeing the emergence of Houses of Prayer all over the earth with prayer going up 24/7. Prayer is calling for the Bridegroom's return, and for the Bride to be made ready. Prayers that are storming the heavens and binding the "strong men", declaring and decreeing God's Kingdom rule in every jurisdiction. This is what we call Kingdom Advancing Prayer. This kind of prayer is released from the heart of Father God into the hearts of His people, as we seek for His Glory to cover the earth as the waters cover the sea. What a GLORIOUS DAY to be ALIVE and to be in the WILL and PLAN of FATHER GOD! HALLELUJAH!

To Order Contact:
Word Alive Press Inc.
131 Cordite Road • Winnipeg, MB, R3W 1S1 • Canada
Phone: 866-967-3782 • Fax: 800-352-9272

Identifying and Defeating the Jezebel Spirit

I declare to you with the greatest of conviction that we are living in the days when Malachi 4:5-6 is being fulfilled. The Elijah spirit is truly in the earth as the Lord prepares His Church for the return of Jesus and the culmination of all things. However as it was in the days of Elijah of old so it is in these days.

Elijah in his day had to confront and deal with a false spiritual order and government that was established and set up by an evil woman called Jezebel and her spineless husband called Ahab. This spirit is still active in the earth and in the Church; however the Lord is restoring His holy apostles and prophets to identify and destroy this spirit as recorded in Revelation 2:18-23

As you read through the pages of this book it is my prayer that you will be enlightened to the reality of the battle and the strategy the Lord has given us to effect the ultimate victory.

To Order Contact:
Dominion-Life International
Box 44592 Garden Park
Vancouver, BC, V5M 4R8, Canada
Phone: 604-953-1087 • Fax: 604-953-1085
Or visit our website at http://www.dominion-life.org

Printed in the United States
1422600003B/1-51